The

Girls

Bloomsbury Methuen Drama
An imprint of Bloomsbury Publishing Plc

B L O O M S B U R Y

LONDON · OXFORD · NEW YORK · NEW DELHI · SYDNEY

Bloomsbury Methuen Drama
An imprint of Bloomsbury Publishing Plc

50 Bedford Square	1385 Broadway
London	New York
WC1B 3DP	NY 10018
UK	USA

www.bloomsbury.com

Bloomsbury is a registered trademark of Bloomsbury Publishing Plc

First published 2016

© Theresa Ikoko, 2016

British Library Cataloguing-in-Publication Data
A catalogue record for this book is available from the British Library

ISBN: PB: 978-1-3500-0509-9
ePub: 978-1-3500-0511-2
ePDF: 978-1-3500-0510-5

Library of Congress Cataloging-in-Publication Data
A catalog record for this book is available from the Library of Congress

Cover image: Richard Lakos

Typeset by Country Setting, Kingsdown, Kent CT14 8ES

HighTide
Soho Theatre
and Talawa Theatre Company present

GIRLS

by Theresa Ikoko

Originally presented at HighTide Festival
and at Soho Theatre in 2016 produced by
HighTide, Soho Theatre and Talawa Theatre Company.

HighTide, Soho Theatre
and Talawa Theatre Company present

Girls

by Theresa Ikoko

Cast

Haleema	**Anita-Joy Uwajeh**
Ruhab	**Yvette Boakye**
Tisana	**Abiola Ogunbiyi**

Creative Team

Director	**Elayce Ismail**
Set and Costume Designer	**Rosanna Vize**
Lighting Designer	**Andy Purves**
Sound Designer	**Richard Hammarton**
Casting Director	**Nadine Rennie CDG**
Production Manager	**Sarah Cowan**
Stage Manager	**Tanith MacKenzie**
Deputy Stage Manager	**Mica Taylor**

Cast Biographies

ANITA-JOY UWAJEH | Haleema

Theatre credits include: *Fury* (Soho Theatre); *We Wait in Joyful Hope* (Theatre 503); *Othello* (Smooth Faced Gents/Edinburgh Festival); *Titus Andronicus* (Smooth Faced Gents, Greenwich Theatre); *Gone Too Far, A Day at the Racists, Lady From the Sea, Ivanov, Threesome, Twelfth Night, The White Devil, Iphigenia in Aulis* (Drama Centre); *Bow Down* (The Opera Group); *Every Human Creature* (Southwark Playhouse Young Company).

Film credits include: *Agent 47* (Fox). TV credits include: *Lucky Man* (Carnival for Sky 1); *Not Safe for Work* (Clerkenwell Films for Channel 4); *Transporter* (Atlantique Productions).

YVETTE BOAKYE | Ruhab

Yvette trained in acting at the Oxford School of Drama. Since completing the three-year course she has gone on to perform at Hampstead Theatre, Soho Theatre (for Writers Avenue), Arcola Theatre (for Miniaturists 50), Drill Hall, Blenheim Palace (Oxford School of Drama), Etcetera Theatre (*Skin Like Butter*) and Latitude Festival. Her first written play, which she also directed, was shown at York Gardens in summer 2016.

ABIOLA OGUNBIYI | Tisana

Abiola trained at the Emerald Music School and ArtsEd, London.

Theatre includes: *The Book of Mormon* (Prince of Wales Theatre); *Mamma Mia!* (Prince of Wales/Novello Theatres); *Travels with My Aunt* (Chichester Festival Theatre); *Sweeney Todd* (West Yorkshire Playhouse/ Royal Exchange Theatre); *Peter Pan* (Watermill Theatre); *Hairspray* (Cork Opera House); *Hair* (European tour); *Soho Cinders* (Gala Concert, Queen's); *Little Shop of Horrors* (Kilworth House); *The Merchant of Venice* (National Centre for the Performing Arts, Beijing).

Television includes: *2008 Beijing Olympics Closing Ceremony, Building the Olympic Dream* (BBC).

Abiola is also a writer, director and producer. Her work includes *The Danish Girl* (short film, official selection at the Hackney Attic Film Festival) and her YouTube vlog *Abiola Is My Name*.

Creative Team Biographies

THERESA IKOKO | Writer

Theresa Ikoko studied psychology as an undergraduate and a Master's in Criminology and Criminal Justice. She has had a variety of roles in prisons, secure settings and social inclusion/community engagement projects. She now works in the area of gangs and serious youth violence. *Girls* is Theresa's first full-length play, and won the Alfred Fagon Award 2015, was joint winner of the George Devine Award 2016, and was shortlisted, with judges' commendation, at the Verity Bargate Award 2015.

ELAYCE ISMAIL | Director

Elayce Ismail was awarded the JP Morgan Award for Emerging Directors 2014/2015, under which she was Resident Director at the National Theatre Studio and directed Andrew Whaley's *The Rise and Shine of Comrade Fiasco* at the Gate Theatre. Prior to this, she was a Jerwood Assistant Director at the Young Vic in 2013. Elayce was a founder and Co-Artistic Director/Producer of Offstage Theatre from 2005–2009, is an Associate Artist of the National Youth Theatre and trained at LISPA.

Direction includes: *The Iphigenia Quartet: Chorus, The Rise and Shine of Comrade Fiasco* (Gate Theatre); *Stay Another Song, Simpatico* (Young Vic); *The Lost Ring* (NT/Deutsches Theater Berlin); *Nanjing* (The Yard); *Treasure Island: Making a Scene; Girls* (Alfred Fagon Award/Black Plays Series readings, NT); *Struggle* (Talawa Firsts/London and Bristol Somali Festivals); *Bed and Breakfast* (Brighton Fringe Festival & tour).

Associate/assistant Direction: *The Virtues of Things* (Royal Opera House); *The Sound of Yellow, A Season in the Congo* (Young Vic); *Coming Home* (Arcola Theatre).

Puppetry: *Dr Korczak's Example* (Unicorn Theatre); *Fast Burn* (Kneehigh/NYT).

Performance: *The Magic Flute* (Complicite/ENO); *Ring-a-Ding-Ding* (Oily Cart); *In a Pickle* (Oily Cart/RSC).

ROSANNA VIZE | Set and Costume Designer

Rosanna Vize is a freelance theatre designer. She graduated from Bristol Old Vic Theatre School in 2013 when she became one of twelve finalists for the Linbury Prize for Stage Design.

Previous work includes: *The Rise and Shine of Comrade Fiasco* (Gate Theatre); *Infinite Lives* by Chris Goode, *Coastal Defences, Banksy: the Room in the Elephant* by Tom Wainwright (Tobacco Factory Theatre); *The Tinder Box, Joan of the Stockyards, A Thousand Seasons Passed, Talon, The Last Days of Mankind, Dark Land Lighthouse* (Bristol Old Vic); *Measure for Measure, Black*

Sheep (Oxford School of Drama); *Edward Gant's Amazing Feats of Loneliness* by Anthony Neilson, *The Wicked Lady* by Bryony Lavery (Bristol Old Vic Theatre School); *A Midsummer Night's Dream* (Garsington Opera/RSC); *Noye's Fludde* (Orchestival in association with Kneehigh Theatre); *Don Giovanni* (Hampstead Garden Opera); *The Picture of John Gray* (Old Red Lion); Howard Barker Double Bill (Arcola Theatre).

Current work includes: *Diary of a Madman* by Al Smith (Gate Theatre); *FUP* by Simon Harvey (Kneehigh Theatre); *After October* (Finborough Theatre). Rosanna has also worked regularly as an assistant to Anna Fleischle and was the resident assistant designer for the Royal Shakespeare Company 2014–2015.

ANDY PURVES | Lighting Designer

Andy is a lighting designer working in theatre, circus and educational projects. He trained in sound and lighting engineering at the University of Derby and has an MA in lighting design and theatre-making from Central School of Speech and Drama.

Lighting designs include projects made with: Frantic Assembly; Old Vic New Voices; Royal College of Music; The Freedom Theatre, Palestine; Theatre Royal, Plymouth; The Watermill, Newbury; The Nuffield, Southampton; The Unicorn; The National Centre for Circus Arts; The Sherman, Cardiff; Young Vic; Eastern Angles; New Perspectives; Inspector Sands; Spymonkey; Barbican, London; Sydney Theatre Company; Caroline Horton; Northampton Royal; Stan Won't Dance; Tamasha; Brighton Festival; Tom Adams; Annie Siddons; La Soirée/La Clique; Cartoon de Salvo; National Theatres of Wales and Scotland.

Andy is co-convener of SiPA, The Sustainability in Production Alliance, which was launched in 2015. He is committed to cultivating, encouraging and promoting environmentally responsible and sustainable practice across the live production industry.

Andy won a Knight of Illumination Award for his work on Frantic Assembly's *The Believers* in 2014.   www.andypurves.com www.sipa.org.uk

RICHARD HAMMARTON | Sound Designer

Recent theatre credits include: *Much Ado About Nothing, Jumpy* (Theatr Clwyd); *Linda* (Royal Court); *Tomcat* (Papatango); *Crushed Shells and Mud* (Southwark Playhouse); *The Crucible* (Manchester Royal Exchange); *Sunspots, Deposit* (Hampstead Theatre); *Comrade Fiasco* (Gate Theatre); *Grimm Tales* 2 (Bargehouse, Oxo Tower Wharf); *Beached* (Marlowe Theatre/Soho Theatre); *Ghost from a Perfect Place* (Arcola); *The Crucible* (Old Vic); *Dealer's Choice* (Royal and Derngate).

Television credits include: *Ripper Street* Series 1 and 2 (BBC); *Agatha Christie's Marple: The Secret Of Chimneys*, Series 3–4 (ITV); *No Win No Fee, Sex 'n' Death, Wipeout, The Ship* (BBC).

Soho Theatre is a major creator of new theatre, comedy and cabaret. Across our three different spaces we curate the finest live performance we can discover, develop and nurture. Soho Theatre works with theatremakers and companies in a variety of ways, from full producing of new plays, to co-producing new work, working with associate artists and presenting the best new emerging theatre companies that we can find. We have numerous writers and theatre makers on attachment and under commission, young writers and comedy groups, and we read and see hundreds of shows a year – all in an effort to bring our audience work that amazes, moves and inspires.

'Soho Theatre was buzzing, and there were queues all over the building as audiences waited to go into one or other of the venue's spaces. [The audience] is so young, exuberant and clearly anticipating a good time.'
Guardian

Within our Dean Street home and on tour around the UK and internationally we attract over 220,000 audience members a year. We produced, co-produced or staged over forty new plays in the last twelve months.

Our social enterprise business model means that we maximise value from Arts Council and philanthropic funding; we actually contribute more to government in tax and NI than we receive in public funding.

sohotheatre.com

Keep up to date: sohotheatre.com/mailing-list
facebook.com/sohotheatre
twitter.com/sohotheatre
youtube.com/sohotheatre

Registered Charity No: 267234

Soho Theatre, 21 Dean Street, London W1D 3NE
Admin 020 7287 5060   Box Office 020 7478 0100

Supported using public funding by
ARTS COUNCIL
ENGLAND
LOTTERY FUNDED

Submitting Your Work to Soho Theatre

We make the very best entertaining, challenging, profound new work across a range of live performance genres.

We are the place where emerging and established writers conceive, develop and realise their work.

We want to push the form in a way that delights and inspires our audience.

There are no thematic, political or philosophical constraints and though we love to produce a writers' first play, we have no objection to your second, third or fiftieth.

We are looking for unique and unheard voices – from all backgrounds, attitudes and places.

We want to make things you've never seen before.

If you would like to submit a script to us please send it as a PDF or Word attachment to **submissions@sohotheatre.com**.

Your play will go directly to our artistic team.

We consider every submission for production or for further development opportunities. Although there are a limited number of slots on our stages, we engage with writers throughout the year through workshops, readings, notes sessions and other opportunities.

Thank You

Soho Theatre is a charity and social enterprise. We are supported by Arts Council England and we put every £1 we make back into our work. Our supporters are key to our success and we are immensely grateful for their support. We would like to thank Soho Theatre Friends and Members as well as our supporters:

Principal Supporters
Nicholas Allott
Hani Farsi
Jack and Linda Keenan
Amelia and Neil Mendoza
Lady Susie Sainsbury
Carolyn Ward
Jennifer and Roger Wingate

The Soho Circle
Celia Atkin
Moyra Doyle
Stephen Garrett
Hedley and Fiona Goldberg
Jon Grant
Tim Macready
Suzanne Pirret

Corporate Supporters
Adnams Southwold
Bargate Murray
Bates Wells & Braithwaite
Cameron Mackintosh Ltd
EPIC Private Equity
Financial Express
Fosters
The Groucho Club
John Lewis Oxford Street
Latham & Watkins LLP
Lionsgate UK
The Nadler Hotel
Oberon Books Ltd
Overbury Leisure
Quo Vadis
Richmond Associates
Soho Estates
Soundcraft

Trusts & Foundations
The Andor Charitable Trust
Backstage Trust
Bertha Foundation
Boris Karloff Charitable

Foundation
Bruce Wake Charitable Trust
The Buzzacott Stuart Defries Memorial Fund
The Chapman Charitable Trust
The Charles Rifkind and Jonathan Levy Charitable Settlement
Cockayne – Grants for the Arts and The London Community Foundation
The Coutts Charitable Trust
The David and Elaine Potter Foundation
The D'Oyly Carte Charitable Trust
The Ernest Cook Trust
The Edward Harvist Trust
The Eranda Foundation
Esmée Fairbairn Foundation
The Fenton Arts Trust
The Foundation for Sport and the Arts
The Foyle Foundation
The Goldsmiths Company
Harold Hyam Wingate Foundation
Help A London Child
Hyde Park Place Estate Charity
The Ian Mactaggart Trust
The Idlewild Trust
John Ellerman Foundation
John Lewis Oxford Street Community Matters Scheme
John Lyon's Charity
The John Thaw Foundation
JP Getty Jnr Charitable Trust

The Kobler Trust
The Mackintosh Foundation
The Mohamed S. Farsi Foundation
The Peggy Ramsay Foundation
The Rose Foundation
The Royal Victoria Hall Foundation
St Giles-in-the-Fields and William Shelton Educational Charity
The St James's Piccadilly Charity
Teale Charitable Trust
The Theatres Trust
The Thistle Trust
Unity Theatre Charitable Trust
The Wolfson Foundation

Soho Theatre Best Friends
Matthew and Brooke Barzun
Nick Bowers
Prof Dr Niels Brabandt
Barbara Broccoli
Richard Collins
David and Beverly Cox
Miranda Curtis
Norma Heyman
Isobel and Michael Holland
Beatrice Hollond
David King
Lady Caroline Mactaggart
Hannah Pierce
Amy Ricker
Ian Ritchie and Jocelyne van den Bossche
Ann Stanton
Alex Vogel
Sian and Matthew Westerman
Mark Whiteley

Gary Wilder
Alexandra Williams
Hilary and Stuart Williams

Soho Theatre Dear Friends

Nick Allan
Christiane Amanpour
Ken Anderson
David Aukin
Natalie Bakova
James Boyle
Rajan Brotia
James Brown
Simon Brown, Founder
The ESTAS Group
Lisa Bryer
Steve Coogan
Fiona Dewar
Cherry and Rob Dickins
Manu Duggal
Chris Evans
Denzil and Renate Fernandez
Dominic Flynn
Jonathan Glanz and Manuela Raimondo
Alban Gordon
Kate Horton
John James
Dede Johnston
Shappi Khorsandi
Jeremy King
Lynne Kirwin
Michael Kunz
David and Linda Lakhdhir
Anita and Brook Land
Jonathan Levy
Patrick Marber
Nick Mason and Annette
Lynton Mason
Aoife O'Brien
Adam Morley
Aoife O'Brien
Rick Pappas
Natasha Parker
Leanne Pollock
Lauren Prakke
Phil and Jane Radcliff

John Reid
James Robertson
Sue Robertson
Alexandra Sears
Robert & Melanie Stoutzker
Dominic and Ali Wallis
Garry Watts
Gregg Wilson
Andrea Wong
Matt Woodford
Henry Wyndham
Christopher Yu

Soho Theatre Good Friends

Oladipo Agboluaje
James Atkinson
Jonathan and Amanda Baines
Uri Baruchin
Antonio Batista
Alex Bridport
Jesse Buckle
Indigo Carnie
Paul Carpenter
Chris Carter
Sharon Eva Degen
Michelle Dietz
Niki di Palma
Jeff Dormer
Geoffrey and Janet Eagland
Edwina Ellis
Peter Fenwick
Gail and Michael Flesch
Sue Fletcher
Daniel and Joanna Friel
James Flitton
Cyrus Gilbert-Rolfe
Eva Greenspan
Doug Hawkins
Etan Ilfeld
John Ireland
Fran Jones
Susie Lea
Simon Lee
Tom Levi
Ian Livingston

Nicola Martin
Kathryn Marten
Amanda Mason
Neil Mastrarrigo
Gerry McGrail
Andrew and Jane McManus
Mr and Mrs Roger Myddelton
Dr Tara Naidoo
Max Nicholson
Alan Pardoe
Edward Pivcevic
Sadia Quyam
Stephanie Ressort
Barry Serjent
Ed Smith
Hari Sriskantha
Francis and Marie-Claude Stobart
Sam Swallow
Lesley Symons
Sue Terry
Gabriel Vogt
Anja Weise
Mike Welsh
Matt Whitehurst
Allan Willis
Liz Young

Soho Theatre has the support of the Channel 4 Playwrights' Scheme sponsored by Channel 4 Television.

Also kindly supported by Westminster City Council West End Ward Budget and the London Borough of Waltham Forest.

We would also like to thank those supporters who wish to remain anonymous.

This list is correct as of August 2016.

Talawa Theatre Company
Thirty years of celebrating Black theatre

'I believe theatre is vital to our lives, it's important to see oneself reflected in the arts, and at Talawa this is our aim.'

Michael Buffong,
Artistic Director, Talawa Theatre Company

Talawa is the UK's primary Black-led theatre company. We began our 30th anniversary year by announcing the co-production of *King Lear* starring Don Warrington, with the Royal Exchange Theatre Manchester, and in association with Birmingham Repertory Theatre.

King Lear consolidated our record of producing work which shines a much-needed spotlight on Black artists, creating theatre for diverse audiences across the country and effecting representation for Black artists and creatives in mainstream theatre.

Talawa has mounted more than fifty award-winning productions over our thirty-year history. Recent productions have included the critically acclaimed production of *King Lear* by William Shakespeare, *All My Sons* by Arthur Miller (Royal Exchange Theatre, UK tour), *Moon on a Rainbow Shawl* by Errol John (National Theatre, UK tour) and *God's Property* by Arinze Kene (Soho Theatre, UK tour).

Talawa was founded in 1986 by Black artists and activists Yvonne Brewster OBE, Mona Hammond, Carmen Munroe and Inigo Espejel, in order to address the lack of opportunities for Black actors on British stages. The vision was to diversify the theatre industry; making it fully representative of the UK's population. Today, led by Artistic Director Michael Buffong, Talawa dedicates its resources to creating high quality touring productions and to developing Black artists. The company enables this by:

- producing one national touring production a year
- developing a canon of new Black British plays through commissioning, training and giving dramaturgical feedback through the free to use script reading service

- supporting the careers of over 100 Black theatre artists, backstage staff and administrators annually by offering training, mentoring, and a chance to develop and present creative ideas using theatre as a learning and/or personal development tool in schools, community groups and in businesses

Support Us

Talawa is a registered charity. All the money that we earn or raise is reinvested back into the work that we do. We receive the support of trusts and foundations including Esmée Fairbairn Foundation, Paul Hamlyn Foundation and the Martin Bowley Charitable Trust. Talawa Theatre Company is an Arts Council England National Portfolio Organisation. With your help we can continue to tour engaging and powerful theatre for audiences across the UK and support the next generation of Black artists to create dynamic new work which reflects the UK today.

Talawa was recently awarded the Catalyst Evolve fund from Arts Council England. This means that for every £1 we fundraise* the Arts Council will match it, so we will effectively double our money.

*ACE will match any income raised up to a total of £105,000

Visit **talawa.com/support-us** to find out how you can support us.

Registered charity No 2005971

Talawa Theatre Company

Artistic Director   Michael Buffong
Executive Director   Natasha Bucknor
Administrator   Mimi Findlay
Finance Manager   Zewditu Bekele
Producer, Participation & Learning   Gail Babb
Marketing and Communications Manager   Sanjit Chudha
Literary Associate   Jane Fallowfield

Board
Derek Brown, Heather Clark-Charrington, Greg Hersov (Chair), Jim Janus Kenworth, Nadia Latif, Sue Mayo, Viloshini Sinden, Don Warrington, Colin Washington.

Patrons
Nonzo Anozie and Michaela Coel

Contact Us
Get involved at Talawa. Visit us at **www.talawa.com** or at **hq@talawa.com**

HIGH TIDE

A MAJOR PLATFORM FOR NEW PLAYWRIGHTS

HighTide is a theatre company.

We produce new plays in an annual festival in Aldeburgh, Suffolk and on tour.

Our programming influences the mainstream. Our work takes place in the here and now.

HighTide: Adventurous theatre for adventurous people.

HIGH TIDE

2016

A DECADE OF INFLUENCING THE MAINSTREAM

Our tenth anniversary season commenced with the world premiere of Anders Lustgarten's **The Sugar-Coated Bullets of the Bourgeoisie** at Arcola Theatre ahead of opening HighTide Festival 2016.

Rob Drummond's **In Fidelity** premiered at the Traverse Theatre before opening HighTide Festival 2016.

HighTide Festival 2016 premiered new works by Theresa Ikoko, Elinor Cook, Anders Lustgarten and Rob Drummond as well as a special HighTide Anniversary production of **The Path**, featuring writing by Luke Barnes, EV Crowe, Vickie Donoghue, Thomas Eccleshare, Ella Hickson, Harry Melling and Vinay Patel.

Theresa Ikoko's debut production **Girls** transferred to Birmingham Repertory Theatre and Soho Theatre following its premiere at HighTide Festival 2016.

Elinor Cook's **Pilgrims** transferred to the Yard Theatre and Theatr Clwyd following its premiere at HighTide Festival 2016.

Al Smith's seminal play **Harrogate** will receive its London premiere at the Royal Court Theatre ahead of a national tour with house in Autumn 2016.

Our final 10th anniversary production, **The Brolly Project**, will premiere at the Young Vic Theatre in February 2017 with Look Left Look Right and the Young Vic Theatre.

For full details, visit hightide.org.uk

H|GH T|DE

24a St John Street, London, EC1M 4AY
0207 566 9765 - hello@hightide.org.uk - hightide.org.uk

H|GH T|DE

WE NEED YOUR SUPPORT

There are very talented young playwrights in the UK, and if they are lucky they will find their way to the HighTide Festival Theatre season in Suffolk. I hope you will join me in supporting this remarkable and modest organisation. With your help HighTide can play an even more major role in the promoting of new writing in the UK.

— Lady Susie Sainsbury, Backstage Trust

HighTide is a registered charity and we could not champion the next generation of theatre artists and create world-class productions for you without ticket sales, fundraising, sponsorship and public investment.

To undertake our work this year we need to raise over £750,000.

We need your help to make these targets. You can show your support by: making a donation; buying Festival tickets; recommending the Festival to your friends; donating your time to help work on the Festival; writing to your local councillor and MPs about how much you value the HighTide Festival.

If you would like to discuss making a donation to HighTide, please speak to freddie@hightide.org.uk or call on 0207 566 9765.

We are thankful to all of our supporters, without whom our work simply would not take place.

Leading Partner: Lansons

Major Funder: Backstage Trust

Trusts and Foundations
Boris Karloff Charitable Foundation; Cockayne Grants for the Arts; Esmeé Fairbairn Foundation; Harold Hyam Wingate Foundation; London Community Foundation; Mackintosh Foundation; Martin Bowley Charitable Trust; The Old Possum's Practical TrustParham Trust; Peter Wolff Trust.

Individual Supporters
Sam Fogg; Clare Parsons and Tony Langham; Tony Mackintosh and Criona Palmer; Lady Susie Sainsbury; Albert and Marjorie Scardino.

Corporate Sponsors
John Clayton and Bishops Printers United Agents.

HIGH TIDE

LANSONS CONGRATULATES HIGHTIDE ON THEIR 10TH ANNIVERSARY

Since 2008, HighTide and Lansons have celebrated a year-on-year partnership that is unique. Lansons is a highly regarded reputation management and PR firm whose work is largely split between building reputations for organisations growing rapidly in the market and protecting reputations of those facing challenges. This partnership was awarded three silver Corporate Engagement Awards in 2016, and has been featured in the Evening Standard and The Guardian as an example of innovative collaboration between a business and an arts charity.

Lansons donates office space, meeting rooms, reception services and IT support year-round to HighTide, which allows them to fully re-invest all of their earned income and charitable support straight into their work. HighTide offers Lansons the opportunity to engage with the culture sector by attending their productions.

Both HighTide and Lansons are proud of this mutually beneficial relationship, and hope that by being transparent about the nature of it, more businesses and charities will endeavour to explore working together.

LANSONS
Advice Ideas Results

www.lansons.com

Acknowledgements

Thanks and love: Ms Jenny Payne, Mrs Kumi-Mensah, Mr Martin, Ms Whyte, Ola Animashawun, Michael Buffong, Jane Fallowfield, Ikenna Obiekwe, Nina Steiger, Abigail Gonda, Steve Marmion, Steve Atkinson, Ayo, Pam, Chuks, Tracy, Ola, Corinne, Ihuaku, Daniel Bailey, Somalia Seaton, Bevan Celestine, Elayce Ismail, Nadine Rennie, Yvette Boakye, Abiola Ogunbiyi, Anita Joy Uwajeh, Faith Alabi, Cherrelle Skeete, Joan Iyola, David Smart, all at HighTide Theatre, all at Talawa Theatre Company, all at Soho Theatre, all at Methuen Drama/ Bloomsbury, board and trustees at George Devine Award, Alfred Fagon Award and Verity Bargate Award, and all family, friends and professionals who have read, listened, encouraged and supported.

Special thank you and love: Chuka Ikoko and Moses Fadairo.

Girls

To the unseen, underestimated, forgotten,
ignored, abandoned and lonely survivors –
from the extraordinary to the everyday.

Characters

Tisana
Haleema
Ruhab

Scene One

Exterior. Hot. Humid. **Haleema**, **Ruhab** *and* **Tisana** *are sweaty.* **Tisana** *does* **Ruhab***'s hair.*

Tisana   – But how did you know?

Ruhab   I don't know, you just do.

Tisana   What does it *feel* like?

Haleema   Oh. For Christ sake, just answer her before I tear my ears off and beat her with –

Ruhab (*to* **Tisana**)   – It's just, you know . . . like that rumbling feeling in your stomach when you ride a bike down the hill too fast.

Tisana   Mama says girls shouldn't ride bikes, that I might scrape my knee.

Haleema   And heaven forbid you scrape your knee. Because that is the worst thing that may happen to you . . . clearly.

Ruhab   Leave her. Your mother is right . . . Just like a woman's hair is her crown, her legs are . . . her chariot. Her golden chariot – like Queen Elizabeth's –

Tisana   – Or Cinderella –

Haleema   / Cinderella rode a pumpkin, actually –

Ruhab   / They should be smooth and clean –

Tisana   – And shiny.

She spits in her hands. She rubs her legs.

Haleema (*rubbing her leg, self-conscious*)   Mine aren't.

Tisana   But you're not like a proper gi –

Haleema   – I'm not what?

Ruhab   She just means, you know, you don't care about those things. Like you always say, 'marriage is for –

Ruhab *and* **Tisana**   – women who don't know how to use tools, except for the one between their legs.'

Haleema (*slapping her legs*)   These damn mosquitos are not helping.

Tisana   Don't scratch –

Haleema *scowls at* **Tisana**.

Ruhab   – Tool is such a hard word for your . . . *flower* . . . anyone would think you can use it to open a bottle of Supermalt.

Haleema   If that were the case, I'm sure every man in town would have been petitioning my father for my hand in marriage. One goat and a bottle of palm wine later – Hmph, that my father? Even for a bottle of stout, I'm sure I would certainly have been engaged . . . A long time ago . . . (*To* **Ruhab**.) Even before you.

I mean, after all, a bottle-opener is a man's favourite tool.

Ruhab   True . . . but logistically . . . a *flower* that can tear a metal cap from a bottle's mouth, might not be the most appealing destination for his . . . *banana*.

Tisana *blushes.*

Haleema (*mock disapproval*)   Now look . . . you have embarrassed her . . . Good thing you didn't say *dick*! Or *cock*! Or –

Tisana   – Halle –

Haleema   – And besides, a woman has at least three other places for his . . . *banana*.

Ruhab *and* **Tisana**   Three?!

Ruhab *counts on her fingers. She thinks.*

Ruhab   Yes. You're right.

Haleema   I'd be like his personal pocket knife. (*Demonstrating complex sex positions.*) Flip this way to open a bottle of Guinness after a long day, and this way to –

Tisana   – OK, OK, OK. Please. We get it.

Ruhab *and* **Haleema** *laugh.* **Tisana** *tries not to.*

Tisana *returns to* **Ruhab***'s hair.* **Ruhab** *itches her scalp.* **Tisana** *catches* **Ruhab***'s hand.*

Tisana   I wish you brought the ring.

Haleema   For what?

Tisana   I don't know. I like looking at it. We could play with it. Make stories about weddings. You know. Fun things like that.

Haleema (*insincerely*)   Sounds like a blast.

Tisana   I just mean –

Haleema   – When would she have had time to –

Tisana   – It's nice to have nice things, Halle, that's all . . . I just wish we had one nice thing here.

Ruhab   Me too. I shouldn't have taken it off before bed.

Haleema   You are mourning that cheap piece of –

Tisana   – It's the sentiment that counts.

Ruhab   It was only temporary anyway . . . until we move to the city. And then Moses said I can pick out any ring I want, from any of the top jewellers.

Tisana   I heard Tiwa Savage got her ring from a jeweller in –

Haleema   – Why limit yourself to the ranks of Tiwa Savage? In fact, let's inquire as to where Beyoncé's ring came from . . . Or even Princess Kate!

Ruhab   Whatever. Hater.

Tisana   What do you think they're all doing now?

Ruhab   Who?

Tisana   Your Moses? . . . My dad? . . . Anyone really.

Ruhab   Well, I bet your dad is holding a prayer meeting. At his house.

She and **Haleema** *become animated. They mimic voices and actions, recreating the atmosphere of* **Tisana**'s *father's church.*

Haleema (*imitating* **Tisana**'s *dad – an energetic, zealous, pentecostal pastor*)   'We are gathered here today – '

Ruhab (*as* **Tisana**'s *dad*)   'Glory be to God.'

Haleema (*as* **Tisana**'s *dad*)   'No weapon fashioned against us!'

Ruhab (*as* **Tisana**'s *dad*)   'Somebody say amen!'

Ruhab, **Tisana** *and* **Haleema**   'Amen'

Ruhab (*loudly, as* **Tisana**'s *dad*)   'Halleluyah'

Ruhab *and* **Haleema**   'Praise!' –

Tisana   – (*looking around, nervous*)   Shhhhh . . .

They freeze. They wait. Nothing. **Ruhab** *mouths 'Sorry'. They wait another moment.*

Haleema   Hauwa is probably shaking in the corner.

Ruhab   Jumping up and down.

Tisana   Catching the Holy Spirit.

Ruhab *scoffs.*

Haleema (*doubtful*)   The 'Holy Spirit'?

Ruhab (*demonstrating, punctuating every other word with a bounce*) You mean, when she is bouncing her tits up and down so hard, so someone will notice her and finally marry her?

They laugh. **Tisana** *laughs, embarrassed.*

Haleema   And Bawa scuttling around, like a beetle on hot stone, with the offering bowl . . . The invisible boy.

Ruhab (*demonstrating on* **Haleema**)   I once saw Mr Saidu rest his elbow on Bawa's head for the whole sermon.

Haleema *shrugs* **Ruhab** *off.*

Ruhab   He must have thought he was a chair.

Haleema (*as if announcing the title to a horror/superhero film*) Bawa . . . The invisible boy.

Tisana   I feel sorry for him . . . people always bumped into him or tripped over him and then scolded him for being so transparent. He couldn't help that he was see-through.

Haleema   You could definitely still watch TV if he stood in front of it.

She has an idea. She changes the channel on an imaginary TV, using an imaginary remote. **Tisana** *sits/stands in her way.*

Haleema (*imitating her dad, to* **Tisana**)   'Is your daddy a glass maker?'

Ruhab *pushes* **Haleema** *out of the way. She tries to change the channel on the imaginary TV, with the imaginary remote.* **Tisana** *is in her way.*

Ruhab (*imitating her dad, to* **Tisana**)   'Then how do you want me to see the television with your big head in the way?'

Haleema (*bitterness rising*)   'You're always in the way. You bloody girl.

The laughter fades. It is uncomfortable. For a moment.

Tisana (*to* **Ruhab**)   You think Moses is still looking?

Ruhab   Of course.

Haleema (*slapping her leg*)   Bloody mosquitoes. I hate this forest!

Ruhab   Me too. It's filthy. My hair smells so bad.

Tisana *stops playing with* **Ruhab**'s *hair. She smells her hands. She wipes them on* **Ruhab**'s *clothes.*

Tisana   I'm starving. I dreamt, last night, that you both turned into massive tubas of yam.

Ruhab   Of course you did. Instead of you to dream of salad –

Haleema   – Ru –

Ruhab   – What? . . . Carbs . . . You know how many calories is in one portion of – (*To* **Tisana**.) This is the best you've ever looked, let me be honest with you.

Haleema *shakes her head. She laughs a little.*

Ruhab (*to* **Haleema**)   I am just saying. It's one way to remain positive. To see the silver lining on a storm cloud, like she always says.

She pulls her clothes tight. She admires her new trimmer figure.

People pay big money for these kind of results: controlled portions, and all the walking they made us do – *days* of walking – to get to this place . . . We are certainly burning more calories than we are eating.

Tisana   How long do you think we've been here?

Ruhab (*trying to comfort*)   Not too long.

Haleema   Not long enough for them to find us though . . . Or maybe *too* long for them to keep looking.

Ruhab (*to* **Tisana**)   It's not rainy season yet . . . It hasn't even been a month. Don't worry . . . they'll come.

Silence. They think. Sadness, doubt, hopelessness flash across their faces.

Tisana *sings, softly. Under her breath. Something upbeat and fun. She gets louder.* **Ruhab** *and* **Haleema** *soften. They relax.* **Ruhab** *joins in singing.* **Tisana** *does* **Ruhab**'s *hair.*

Haleema *itches her legs. She concentrates on her legs. Concentrating on not singing. Ad libs and harmonies slip from her mouth. She shuts her mouth tighter. She concentrates on her legs.*

They sing, maybe dance a little. Upbeat. Fun.

Sounds of explosions and loud gunfire. Darkness falls. Smoke and dust fill the air.

Scene Two

Exterior. Pitch black.

Tisana   Ru?

Spotlight on **Ruhab**. *She is covered in dust. She coughs.*

Ruhab   T?

Spotlight on **Tisana**. *She is dishevelled.*

Tisana   I'm fine. I can't find Halle!

Ruhab   Halle!

Tisana (*panicking*)   Haleema!

Ruhab   Halle.

Tisana (*tearful*)   I can't find her.

Ruhab   We'll find her.

Tisana   I can't find her. Oh God. Please. Jesus. I can't find her. Please – Halle! Where is she?

Ruhab   Haleema!

Tisana (*screaming*)   Halle!

Ruhab (*spotting something*)   Halle. Halle?

She runs out of her spotlight.

(*To* **Tisana**.) She's here.

Tisana *leaves her spotlight.*

Spotlight on **Haleema**. *She is bundled up. She holds herself, her arms wrapped around her head.* **Ruhab** *grabs* **Haleema**. **Haleema** *jumps.*

Ruhab *notices blood. She searches* **Haleema**'s *body to find the source.*

Ruhab   Halle.

Haleema *doesn't respond. Her eyes are wet. Her lips fold.*

Ruhab   Halle? You're hurt? Show me.

Haleema (*tearful*)   Ru . . . Ru, I can't hear anything.

Tisana   Where are you?

Ruhab (*to* **Tisana**)   Follow my voice.

Haleema   I can't hear. I can't hear anything.

Tisana *finds them.*

Haleema   Ru. I can't hear.

The panic, the shock freezes **Ruhab**.

Tisana *snaps into action. She moves* **Ruhab** *out of the way. She holds* **Haleema**. *She locates the bleeding.*

Tisana (*tearing her clothes and wrapping* **Haleema**'s *arm; almost to herself*)   It's OK. It's fine. You'll be fine. We'll be fine.

Haleema   I can't hear anything, T . . .

Tisana *brings* **Haleema**'s *face close to hers.*

Tisana (*exaggerating her mouth's shapes, shouting*)   It's OK. It was just loud and there's so much dust. Your ears are blocked. That's all.

Ruhab *looks at* **Tisana**. *Doubtful.*

Tisana (*sternly*)   Isn't it, Ru? Just blocked.

Ruhab   Yes, of course.

Tisana (*to* **Haleema**)   We'll wash them out and drip some oil in. That's what Mama does when Mark's ears need a good clean.

Ruhab (*to* **Tisana**)   Oil? From where?

Tisana (*to* **Haleema**)   Come on . . . Take my hand.

Ruhab   Where are we going?

Tisana   I don't know.

Movement is heard. A flashlight approaches. They freeze.

Ruhab (*whispering*)   Let's go. Run.

Tisana (*quickly; uncertain; whispering*)   Where? It's too dark. And she's hurt –

Ruhab (*whispering*)   – Then what do we do? We can't stay here.

Tisana *thinks. Hard. She tries not to panic.*

Tisana (*sudden certainty; whispering*)   Maybe it's someone looking for us – to rescue us. Someone good. We should call them.

She goes to call. **Ruhab** *puts her fingers to* **Tisana**'s *mouth and silences her.*

Ruhab   But what if it's not! What if it's not '*someone good*'? What if it's them, I –

Tisana   – It's OK. We're saved. I'm sure of it.

Ruhab   I want to go home.

Tisana   I know.

Ruhab   What if it's them, T? . . . What if it's them looking for us, to take us away *again*? I can't go with them again. It will kill me, T, I swear to God. I will –

Tisana   – It's OK . . . It will be the army . . . Or maybe Moses . . . It'll be someone here to rescue us. Someone good to save us from the bad – Ru . . . Trust me . . . I promise you.

Ruhab   T –

Tisana (*jumping up, shouting*)   Here. Over here –

Ruhab   – T –

Tisana (*shouting*)   – We're here. Please help us.

Scene Three

Interior. **Tisana** *and* **Haleema** *sew black cloth.* **Ruhab** *enters. It is raining outside and she is drenched.*

Ruhab *dumps down a bag of cassava grain (garri).*

Ruhab   Garri. Again.

Haleema   What?

Tisana   She said garri.

Ruhab   It's filled with ants. *Again.*

Haleema (*gesturing to her ear*)   What? Stop speaking on that side of me.

Tisana (*to* **Haleema**)   I'll look for more oil for your ear today.

Haleema   Don't waste your time. One ear is plenty. (*To* **Ruhab**.) You should start cleaning it . . .

Ruhab   I'd rather starve.

Haleema   You can starve on the day that it's not your turn to clean it.

Ruhab *huffs. She squeezes the water from her clothes and hair.*

Tisana   I guess we have to, at least, thank God for a proper roof . . .

Ruhab *and* **Haleema** *look at* **Tisana**. *In judgement.*

– I just meant, that if there is a cloud anyway, why not paint a silver lining. How would we have survived out there in this rain? And you think the mosquitoes troubled you before? The forest would have been infested. And they were running out of food to feed us in the forest . . .

Ruhab (*sarcasm, throwing a handful of grain in the air*)   Yay. Garri. Woohoo.

Tisana   We dreamt of even garri when we had no food for two days straight. (*To* **Haleema**.) And your arm . . . it would probably be infected . . . That's how that small boy, from that other village died . . . And where else would we have found oil? Like you said, one ear is better than none. We have a roof, and –

Ruhab   – You saw what they did to the people who lived in this village –

I prefer the forest, that's all . . . The air was fresher.

Haleema   It was quieter. Or I liked the sounds . . .

Ruhab   I liked knowing where we were. Not exactly where, I know it's probably millions of miles of trees, and God knows I'd never be able to find my way out but –

Tisana   – I know what you mean . . . I guess it *was* familiar.

Ruhab   It felt like home.

Tisana   Do you remember the stories Aunty Hafsat used to tell about the forest when we were small?

Haleema (*smiling a little*)   Yes.

Ruhab   That the forest was home to a mighty giant, that was once the world's greatest warrior and saviour.

Tisana   And one day a war broke out and the giant –

Haleema   – Womba –

Tisana   – Womba was so filled with disappointment and rage over how the people had turned on each other, that he burst into a ball of fire, as big as the sun –

Ruhab   – As hot as hell and –

Tisana   – And wiped out almost everybody.

Ruhab   So now his spirit is home in the forest, and in every flame, and he watches in judgement, and if there is ever a war like the one before, he will set ablaze every tree, bush and shrub, until the world is one big ball of fire.

Haleema   Well . . . I don't know what he's waiting for then. Womba, are you not seeing this?

Tisana   No one can start a fire in this rain.

Haleema   This place and rain – the invisible, mythical giants don't work, the army doesn't work, the roads don't work. Nothing works when it rains.

Ruhab   I miss the forest.

Tisana   I miss home.

Scene Four

Interior. **Ruhab** *and* **Haleema** *sew.* **Tisana** *cleans the garri.*

Tisana (*closing her eyes*)   Hmmmm . . . something beginning with P.

Ruhab   Person.

Tisana *shakes her head.*

Ruhab   Pot.

Tisana (*pleased with herself*)   Nope.

Haleema (*concentrating on sewing*)   Penis.

Ruhab   For goodness sake, Haleema. I think we have surpassed the dick joke quota for today, don't you? . . . And when did you even see a penis?

Haleema   When we stopped on the road, and that ugly one with the scar went to piss. It was tiny. I could barely *see* anything. So maybe it doesn't even count.

Ruhab   When was that?

Haleema   The road before the first village we saw when we left the forest.

Tisana   We did that section already this morning. I am spying between the well and the farm now.

Haleema   You didn't say.

Tisana   After the first village, we always spy from the well to –

Ruhab   – (*to* **Tisana**)   What was it anyway?

Tisana   You have to guess. This is a very hard one, I can give you a clue. You –

Ruhab   – Purple door.

Tisana   . . . Oh.

Ruhab   You do that one every time.

Haleema   I think we've played this game to death now, yes?

Tisana   There must be more things, from the forest to this place, that we haven't remembered.

Haleema   If we don't remember it how can we spy it –

Tisana   – No, I mean . . . Let me think . . . G . . . Something starting with G.

Ruhab   Green truck.

Tisana   No.

Ruhab   The three-legged goat that that fool ran over.

Haleema (*concentrating on her sewing*)   Scarface is the worst driver.

Ruhab   I still feel sick from all the bumping and twisting. How many days were we in the back of that truck, bouncing around like rubber balls?

Haleema (*still sewing*)   They didn't even let us taste it. After we slept with that thing on top of us for days.

Ruhab   And it stank.

Haleema   And the flies.

Tisana   OK – F.

Ruhab (*to* **Tisana**)   Flat tyre. (*To* **Haleema**.) I can still smell it.

Haleema   Not even a taste. Not even to chew the bones.

Tisana (*to* **Ruhab**)   But which –

Ruhab (*to* **Tisana**)   – Does it matter, the tyre?

Tisana   Yes –

Ruhab   – OK, both. The time our truck got one near the bean farm and the one on that abandoned white car.

Tisana   A.

Haleema   Annoying. As in You. Are. Annoying me. And H for the headache you are giving me. And B for the beating I am very close to giving you.

Ruhab   God. What I would do for a spoon of beans.

Tisana   You think they will share some of the beans they got from that farm?

Haleema   Ha.

Ruhab *digs into the hem of her skirt.*

Ruhab (*to* **Haleema**)   Here, I found some clean cloth, I can wrap your arm for you again tonight. We can clean it properly. The buckets will be overflowing.

Ruhab *and* **Haleema** *sew.* **Tisana** *cleans the garri. They are busy.*

Tisana   I found some clean underwear in one of those boxes. It's mostly old bags and newspapers but –

Haleema   – Ew.

Tisana   What? I didn't say I was going to wear it.

Ruhab (*teasing*)   But you were thinking it . . . –

Haleema   – Or you are wearing it already . . . –

Haleema *and* **Ruhab** *laugh.*

Tisana   – They were warm . . . and dry . . . and not filthy.

Haleema   Don't mind us . . . If any of us had found it first, we'd be wearing them too.

Tisana   Who do you think lived here?

Ruhab   A woman – the knickers.

Tisana   Children?

Haleema   Maybe.

Tisana   Husband?

Ruhab   The newspapers. Probably.

Haleema   Or a woman who wants to know more about the world than which Kardashian's ass is real or inflatable.

Tisana   Do you think they're . . .

Haleema   . . . Probably. The husband. Definitely. They lined them – the husbands – the men – all up . . .

Ruhab   Do you think that's what they did at home? You think *all* −

Tisana   − No . . . It happened too quick . . . There wasn't time.

Haleema   And how long do you think bullets take to burst a heart . . . or a brain . . . ? Many bullets passed by our heads, without us knowing what happened behind us. I saw children shot off their fathers' shoulders. Houses burnt with people hiding insi −

Tisana   − I just mean . . . I saw people running . . . I saw people running until they disappeared from my sight. I saw Mr Mohammed − the tailor's husband − running towards the river. I saw people make it.

Haleema   Why was Mohammed running towards the river? He can't swim. Not that distance, anyway. When have you seen a black man in the Olympics for swimming?

Ruhab   Was he with his wife?

Tisana (*hesitant*)   No . . .

Ruhab   Was she with us?

Tisana   No . . .

Ruhab   Maybe she went a different way.

Ruhab *and* **Haleema** *sew.* **Tisana** *cleans the garri. They busy themselves.*

Haleema   You know I've never seen people so afraid. I saw babies, barely able to walk, by themselves. Where were the parents? Somewhere drunk with fear . . . forgetting they had a child. I saw Christina's baby sister. She was just standing there, and everybody ran past her. Back and forth. Kicking her out of the way like she was a football. She didn't even cry. Or maybe the dust had soaked up her cry . . . I know they were scared. I know there were guns and fire. (*Gripping the black cloth.*) And black flags. And all the things that feel apocalyptic. All the things we know are terrifying . . . But just kicking her? . . . But there's no time. Because bullets are faster than legs. Because hearts and brains were exploding everywhere, like a film. Kicking her back and forth. Trampling on her. Bursting her little body without bullets . . . *fear* . . . Fear killed her . . . not a gun . . .

(*Scoffing.*) All those town meetings . . . For *years* . . . People talking about what they would do, how they would defend the women, the children . . . (*Imitating someone.*) How the 'resistance would be more effective than the entire government's army. So effective that the president will recruit our men and fast track them to Lieutenant.'

Ruhab (*trying to laugh*)   You know Uncle Peter was the chairman of those meetings, and you know he insists that nothing should be discussed while people are sober.

Tisana (*as Uncle Peter*)   'You, girl. Bring me a bottle of stout to lubricate my t'inking t'oughts masheen.'

Ruhab (*trying to laugh, to* **Haleema**)   So what do you expect? They probably don't even remember any plan, if any was discussed at all.

Ruhab *and* **Tisana** *try to laugh.* **Haleema** *does not.*

Haleema   I don't know . . . I just expected that . . . just not that people can − . . . I don't know.

Haleema *and* **Ruhab** *sew.* **Tisana** *watches them. She thinks.*

Tisana   My dad saw me . . . I saw him see me. He turned away from me. He grabbed my little brothers and sisters and ran.

Ruhab   Maybe he −

Tisana   – No . . . He saw me. He looked down. He meant sorry. But what was he supposed to do? They need him. My mama needs him.

Haleema   Did she –

Tisana   – No, of course not . . .

Ruhab   She would have –

Tisana   – She would have screamed. She would have tried to fight . . . They would have killed her . . . or taken her too.

Haleema (*to herself*)   A mother's love is foolish.

Tisana   He grabbed her hand and dragged her away. They hid. I kept my eyes on their hiding place as the trucks pulled away. Praying for my little brother not to sneeze, not to cough – The dust always makes him cough. Praying that they would stop looking for more people to take, or kill. I kept my eyes on their hiding place and covered them with my prayers.

Ruhab   Are they –

Tisana   – I think so . . . I think they're alive . . . I didn't see anyone find them and I kept my eyes on them until we had driven too far to see anything.

Haleema *sews.* **Ruhab** *plays with the thread.* **Tisana** *picks bugs out of the grain.*

Haleema (*to* **Ruhab**)   Does it still smell like fire out there?

Ruhab   A little. Like burning rain.

Tisana   And grilled chicken . . . Burning flesh . . . it smells like grilled chicken.

Ruhab   Yes . . . that smell . . . always in the air, like a barbeque.

Tisana   And the smell of raw meat . . . always in the air, like the rain clouds.

Haleema   They still haven't buried the bodies?

Ruhab   No. I even found bodies in the well . . . so there's no more water to drink when the rain stops.

Tisana   We will be home by the time the rain stops.

Haleema   They leave a trail of fire and flesh. If they followed it – if somebody followed the stench – they would find us.

Ruhab   I saw some new girls today . . . maybe people will come for *them*, people who aren't already tired, and then they will find *us* too . . . One of them looked like Jessica.

Haleema   Oh, well, then we are saved.

Tisana   How do you mean?

Haleema   Because you know her mother is a witch. So she probably has a jar of her hair, or toe nails or blood under her bed. And she will use it to locate her. If she finds her, she finds us. We can all relax now.

Tisana   You don't really believe that do you – that she's a witch?

Haleema   All I know is that she showed up pregnant one day. She has never left the village, and no man has ever entered her home, so please, tell me, where did that baby come from?

Ruhab   And I heard people saying that she didn't let any of the women help her deliver the baby.

Haleema   And how long was she pregnant? . . . It was either five months too short, or two years too long.

Ruhab   No one knows which one came first – pregnancy or obesity.

Haleema   Either way, the numbers do not add up.

They laugh.

Ruhab   Oh, to be honest, I would kiss her mouth and bow down to whatever statue or animal bone she worships, if she was to show up, wave her wand, and −

Tisana   − God forbid!

Haleema   You are forbidding God to save you? Foolish girl. (*To God.*) Please O, God O, I am not with her. I *un*-forbid you.

She shakes out the cloth she has been sewing. It's a flag.

Maybe I can hide a secret message somewhere.

Ruhab   Are you James Bond?

Haleema   Just watch . . . I will get us out of here.

Tisana (*looking at the flag*)   Before you start planning your mission impossible, you should check your spelling. Jihad isn't spelt with a G.

Haleema   Honestly. You are so annoying. I will escape this place, just to get away from you. Even here, you wan' do teacher's pet? They will give you gold star, eh?

Ruhab   Whatever, just be sure to correct it before they come for it. Don't bring trouble for us.

Haleema *sulks. For a moment. She dramatically unpicks the letters she has sewn.*

Tisana and **Ruhab** *look at each other. They try not to laugh.*

Tisana   I'll go and get the buckets.

She exits. She bumps **Haleema** *as she leaves. Playfully.* **Haleema** *reaches to hit her.* **Tisana** *dodges.*

Ruhab and **Haleema** *sew.*

Ruhab   Halle . . .

Haleema (*concentrating on her sewing*)   What?

Ruhab (*changing her mind*)   It's nothing.

She sews.

Haleema   I hate it when you do that.

Ruhab *takes a deep breath.*

Ruhab   One of the new girls said she was sent here from another camp.

Haleema (*disinterested*)   What?

Ruhab   Like, another group . . . Like this one. They took over her village or took her to a village they − whatever − Anyway, she said after some time, they started to divide up the girls.

Haleema   What are you −

Ruhab   − I am trying to tell you − stop − just listen − −

Haleema   − Talk faster. Land your point −

Ruhab   − For the men, or to send them away . . . for other men. That's how she ended up here. They sent some of them here. Because they said this chapter had done good work.

Haleema (*scoffing*)   Like a reward? . . . They're not even fine. They look like donkeys. They should send them back.

Ruhab *rolls her eyes.*

Ruhab   And . . . And . . . She . . . / She said . . .

Haleema   / This girl. Talk now.

Ruhab   That some were sent away as fighters . . . or to . . . bomb.

Haleema   Bomb?

Ruhab   You know . . . (*Demonstrating.*) Boom. Boom. Ahhhh. Ahhhh −

Haleema   − I know what a bomb is −

Ruhab   − They would wear it and −

Haleema   – Stop. Nothing –

Ruhab   – Or what if they even split us up and send –

Haleema   – I said, nothing –

Ruhab   – Hal –

Haleema   – Ru. I told you, I will get us out of here.

She sews.

Don't say anything to T. She won't –

Ruhab   – I know.

Scene Five

Interior. Dark. **Tisana** *and* **Ruhab** *sleep.* **Haleema** *makes/ sharpens something. We can't see what it is. She is careful not to wake* **Tisana** *and* **Ruhab**. *A flashlight, steps/voices pass by outside.* **Haleema** *quickly lies down. She pretends to sleep.*

Scene Six

Interior. **Haleema** *prepares the garri.* **Tisana** *does* **Ruhab***'s hair.*

Haleema   I doubt it.

Tisana   Why not?

Haleema   Because other things must have happened by now.

Tisana   The elections, maybe –

Ruhab   – Maybe Rihanna's pregnant?!

Haleema   Basically, we are old news – literally. I'm sure they are using papers with our pictures on them to block the draught in windows.

Ruhab   Or to make projects for school.

Tisana   Do you think school is open again?

Haleema   Did you see how they left it? Who is going to spend the money to fix that place?

Tisana   The government. They'll fix it.

Haleema *places the food on the table.* **Tisana** *and* **Ruhab** *join her. They eat.*

Haleema   Oh please. It is the president who is '*supervising* this suffering'.

Ruhab (*to* **Tisana**, *pointing to the pile of old newspapers*)   That's what one of those papers said.

Haleema   Half of the government probably don't even know what's going on, and the other half that do are pretending that they don't.

She adopts the demeanour of a government official – proud and pompous. An older man. She stuffs rags in her top to give him a belly. She balls up rags/newspaper and stuffs them down her trousers to give him a trouser bulge. She assesses. She was too generous with the bulge. She reduces it and adds the excess to his belly. She pretends he is at a press conference. He is larger than life. A caricature. She is mocking him. He is the butt of the joke.

(*As the minister.*) 'Good evening gentlewomen and polished men, prestigious officers of press, media and correspondence. For those of you from distinguished, international offices of news and broadcast, I make my introduction, for your pleasure, to you, my name is Mr Collin Rutaku, the illustrious minister of eminent duties of engagement and dialogue and nonsensical affairs.'

Ruhab *adopts the character of a reporter. She sticks her hand up.*

Ruhab (*as reporter*)   'Mr Rutaku, can you update us on how talks are going with the group's leaders?'

Haleema (*as minister*)   'It will be my absolute pleasure, noble gentlewoman. So, to begin with, as many of you may know, telephone reception in some of the places where they are located has not been easy – '

Ruhab (*as reporter*)   – 'But they seem to manage to access the internet fairly consistently.'

She leafs through imaginary sheets of paper.

Haleema (*as minister, stumped*)   'E – erm – eh –'

Ruhab   'Yes, I have a print-out here of their last few days' worth of tweets.'

Haleema (*as minister*)   'Errrr – erm – '

Ruhab (*reading from imaginary print-outs, as reporter*)   – 'Peace be upon you, my brothers and si – '

Haleema (*as minister*)   – 'Em, yes. (*Pointing to* **Tisana**.) You, the fine lady there, with the hair golden like Fanta, do you have a question for me?'

Tisana *adopts reporter character. She blushes. She plays with her hair.*

Tisana (*as reporter*)   'Well . . . – '

Ruhab (*as reporter*)   ' You didn't answer my question' –

Haleema (*as minister*)   – 'Oh, young lady, that is real big, army, powerful, classified stuffs you are talking. Did His Royal Highness, Prime Minister Tony Bush, discuss so openly, while he was defeating them people in the Middle East?'

Ruhab (*as reporter*)   'I wouldn't say defeat – '

Haleema (*as minister*)   – 'Bottom line is this, a day of triumphant jubilation is approaching. Our celebrated President has visited the north and humbled himself – (*Looking at us.*) Hashtag the president of the people – to commune amongst the small people of the villages.'

Tisana (*quietly, as reporter*)   'What about the people that were taken? Do you know where – '

Haleema (*as minister*)   – 'OK, if there is no more questions, we will close it there. (*Looking at* **Tisana** *and* **Ruhab**.) Now remember, hashtag register (*Outlining the number '2' with her finger.*) to vote.'

She poses as the minister. She has a wide smile. Her fingers are in a 'peace' sign. She holds the pose for a few seconds.

The girls eat in silence.

Tisana   Maybe the mercenaries will come . . . the ones we saw driving through the village that time.

Ruhab   Ha. You mean the Chinese boy that smiled at you?

Tisana   No. No. I just mean –

Ruhab (*teasing*)   – You are still thinking about that small-eye boy?

Tisana   I am not! I just mean that they are going to come for us, and they will send them – *maybe*. Those mercenaries are training people, so they must be the best. And they will send the best for us.

Haleema   You think so? These our ministers? . . . (*Quietly.*) Instead of thinking of ways to use this insanity to win votes and make money, they should stop wasting time and just torpedo this entire north.

Tisana *gasps.*

Ruhab   Haleema!

Haleema   It's true. We're going to die here anyway. I'd rather be buried – or my corpse left to rot – with *their* blood splattered all over me, than to die at their hands, or even worse, trying to pass one of their horned and fork-tailed babies through my . . . (*Looking at* **Tisana**.) *flower*.

Tisana   You don't think they would, do you? . . .

Haleema   No, because they don't have the strength in their testiculars, or the money . . . Probably, they have spent it all on expanding their waist and flying in mistresses and prostitutes from Dubai.

Tisana   But what if the Americans come – to help, with their drones, and they forget that we're here, and they mistakenly –

Haleema   – Why would they bother? There is nothing for them here. The Europeans won't bother either, because a million of us dying is still not as bad as a handful of them dying. Bad things are *supposed* to happen here. It is not terrorism when all of us look the same.

Ruhab *grabs the mirror shard. She looks at herself. She fixes her hair. She cleans her face.*

Ruhab (*gesturing between herself and* **Haleema**)   *We* do *not* look the same.

Haleema (*rolling her eyes, ignoring* **Ruhab**)   It is civil war, at the most . . . it is conflict. And it is far away enough for nobody to give a shit. No one's coming. We're old news.

Tisana   No! I don't believe you. People are doing something. People are trying. Maybe the army are planning another mission to save us . . . like before in the forest.

Haleema   Mission? You mean that blunder? Those few men with their stomachs popping out of their uniform? When Scarface collected and marched us from the forest to the trucks, through the fumes and smoke from those useless army men's guns and grenades, how many army uniformed bodies, and even children's bodies, did we step on? '*The army*' just came there to kill themselves, and the people that they were supposed to be saving. Not one, not one of those monsters died. I was hurt worse than any of them.

Tisana   Maybe people are campaigning, like before. Facebook. Twitter.

Haleema   Oh please. Shut up! Why is everyone so bloody obsessed with hashtags? What on earth do you want to do with a hashtag? Can you use it to shoot your way out of here?

She grabs **Tisana***'s face.* **Tisana** *flinches.*

Haleema   To become invisible – like Bawa – and walk past them to escape? Can you drink it like poison and kill yourself, peacefully in your sleep, before they get the chance to practise their new, their most creative, most gruesome murder technique on you? Even if the entire population of China tweeted every day, even if the First Lady of the United States dropped a banner from the White House balcony with your name on it, even if on every red carpet, on every award show, they had to wade through the blood of all that these people have killed in order to get to their seats, do you think an ounce of difference would be made? Do you think they would care enough to do something?

No. The answer is no! We do not matter to anyone!

Haleema *eats in silence.*

Tisana (*to* **Haleema**)   *You* matter to me.

It's OK. When we get home. Everything will be OK.

Scene Seven

Interior. **Tisana** *does* **Ruhab***'s hair.*

Tisana (*to* **Ruhab**)   Don't touch it, I'm going to get the mirror.

She looks for the mirror

Where's the mirror?

She finds the mirror.

She holds the mirror up in front of **Ruhab***.*

Tisana   Ta-da.

Ruhab *admires herself and her hair.*

Ruhab   Looking like this is such a burden. (*To the heavens.*)
Mashallah.

Scene Eight

Interior. **Tisana** *and* **Haleema** *sleep.* **Ruhab** *runs in. She is out of
breath and sweaty.* **Ruhab** *lights a lamp. She sees the blood on her
hands and clothes. She throws up.* **Haleema** *wakes.*

Haleema (*groggy, disoriented*)   Ru?

She watches **Ruhab** *for a moment. She is confused from the sleep.*

Haleema   What − . . . Ru?

Ruhab *looks at* **Haleema**. *She sees the horror on* **Haleema**'s
face. She follows **Haleema**'s *eyes to her own bloodstained hands and
clothes.*

Ruhab (*quickly*)   It's not mine.

Haleema   What?

Ruhab   I fell − It's too dark − I tripped over those boys −
from this morning . . .

She throws up.

They were still warm.

She wipes at herself, hard. Hysterically. **Haleema** *gets up quickly. She
is careful not to wake* **Tisana**.

Haleema   It's OK. It's OK. Take it off. I'll wash it.

Ruhab *undresses.* **Haleema** *takes* **Ruhab**'s *clothes and quietly
pours water from the rain bucket into another bucket.* **Tisana** *sleeps.*
Haleema *washes* **Ruhab**'s *clothes.* **Ruhab** *sits in her underwear.
She is uncomfortable. She shivers. It isn't cold.*

Haleema   Am I supposed to ask?

Ruhab *says nothing.* **Haleema** *stares at her. She waits.*

Ruhab   What?

Haleema   Where you were coming from . . .

Ruhab   Do you think it will dry before morning?

Haleema   Ru?

Ru –

Ruhab   – I don't want . . . I don't want to be sent away . . .
What if it's worse with another – at another camp, or what if
they start sending girls to b –

Haleema   – I told you. I will get us out of –

Ruhab   – Haleema . . . Come on.

Haleema   So where were you?

Ruhab   Out back . . . with Ishy –

Haleema   *Ishy?*

Ruhab   The new one. With the limp. The one patrolling.

He's been helping to teach me things . . . Prayers. Ayahs.

Haleema   What?

Tisana *stirs. They pause. They wait.* **Tisana** *is still.*

(*Quieter.*) He's – They –

Ruhab   – No – He's not like them – He's nice – I mean . . .
He's – I – We – . . .

She looks away, embarrassed. **Haleema** *stares at* **Ruhab**. **Ruhab** *is uncomfortable. She feels judged, exposed.*

Ruhab   He's not like them, I mean.

Haleema   *They* are *all* monsters –

Ruhab   – He's trying to help. He doesn't want to be here either.

Haleema *scoffs.*

Ruhab   He had no choice.

Just like *us.*

He says they will start calling us to prayers soon, and that if we learn well, we might get special treatment and maybe they won't . . .

She pulls out a small prayer book from her underwear. She hands it to **Haleema**, *who is reluctant to take it.*

Ruhab   I can show you. I wanted to learn, so I could show you and T. That's why I was meeting with him. So I can – we can . . .

Maybe this can be a way to just get along here . . .

Just until you figure out your plan . . .

Scene Nine

Interior. **Haleema** *and* **Ruhab** *huddle around* **Tisana**. *They tear rags and soak them in rain water. They clean and press* **Tisana**'s *wounds and bruises.*

Ruhab   I know they didn't get my good side.

Haleema   They weren't shooting a music video. You will not be getting any awards for your appearance in it.

Ruhab   I'm just saying, they will send it to the news, YouTube even . . . Millions will see.

Haleema   I think the last thing people watching will be thinking is, 'It's a shame that this video of hostages wasn't shot from a different angle. That girl there, that one in particular, out of all of them, she would definitely have looked better from the other side.'

Ruhab   Whatever. Hater.

Haleema   So shallow.

Ruhab   Well then, I'm sure you don't care that your lips have been dry all morning.

Haleema *quickly covers her mouth. She licks her lips.*

Ruhab   Ha. Who's shallow now?

She and **Tisana** *laugh at* **Haleema**.

Ruhab   See, T, if you didn't have all these wounds, if you just do like us, they would let you be in the videos, and then maybe your parents would see you and they would know you're safe.

Tisana   If they saw me like that, head covered like that, they wouldn't even recognise me.

Ruhab *and* **Haleema** *tend to* **Tisana**'s *wounds*.

Tisana (*flinching*)   Sss. Ow.

Ruhab   Careful. Halle.

Haleema   She should stop moving then.

Ruhab   You're too heavy-handed.

Haleema (*feigning sadness*) It's not my fault, I didn't have a mother to do these things for me as a child. I never learnt the ways of a delicate, womanly touch, like yours.

Ruhab (*laughing*) Boo-hoo, poor you.

Haleema (*to* **Ruhab**) Heartless bitch. (*To* **Tisana**.) And I'm supposed to be the insensitive one.

Tisana (*through the laughter*) Ow. Ow.

Ruhab Haleema! Careful!

Tisana It's OK, it's not you, everything just hurts.

Haleema And you know she's extra soft . . . like butter.

Tisana (*squirming*) OK, girls. That's enough now. Please.

Ruhab *gathers the rags. She rinses them out in the water. The water is pink with blood. She spreads them out to dry.* **Haleema** *settles down to pick bugs out of a bag of garri.* **Tisana** *looks in the mirror.*

Tisana My mum will kill me if I have scars when I get home.

Haleema *looks at* **Ruhab**. **Ruhab** *looks at* **Haleema** *as if to say, 'Don't'.* **Haleema** *cleans the garri.*

Ruhab Are you sure you don't want to just come with us today?

It's really not bad at all. I promise. It's actually quite nice to get out for a bit, and see other people . . . On the way to prayer, one of the new girls catches us up on *Big Brother*. She was actually watching it, when they took her.

It's just praying . . . Does it matter whether you call him Jehovah or Allah? I don't think God cares. He doesn't care what name —

Tisana   – Ru, it's different for you, you didn't grow up how I did.

Ruhab   I went to the same church you did –

Tisana   – But you went to mosque with your mama also, so –

Ruhab   – So I'm probably the most qualified. Trust me, it's the *same* God.

Tisana   I just don't want to disappoint my father.

Ruhab   Do you think he would care whether you said a few prayers a couple of times a day, to stop them from flogging you like a thief in the market? . . . It's the same God.

Haleema   She's right. Sort of . . . This, all of this, it has nothing to do with God. Not the one you think you believe in, not the one they think they are serving, not anyone's God! How many wars have been waged, and bloodshed in '*God's*' name? You think God attended any of them, you think he cheered for the winner? They even killed Jesus, in the name of '*God*'. He, She, whatever God is, He is not that . . . and He is not this.

Ruhab   You have no skin left on your back, Tisana. I'm begging you. Please. Just come.

Tisana   It's about honour. My father . . . He's very big on honour . . . You guys wouldn't understand . . .

Ruhab   Because my father isn't honourable?

Tisana   No, I just – I just meant that I *know* he wouldn't want –

Ruhab   – Well, he's not here, Tisana! You have to start making your own decisions now. We have to grow up. We can't be children any more.

Did you know that this country was once part of a caliphate, anyway? That lasted six centuries? They only want to revive

the glory days of the medieval empires, before the West
divided Africa up like children fighting over their father's will.

Haleema   Do you even know what any of that means? You
sound like you're shitting a dictionary.

Ruhab (*ignoring* **Haleema**)   There are so many things that
we don't really know . . . that we don't learn in school. That
they are teaching us. It's not true that they say girls should be
married and *not* educated . . . just that we should learn things
that matter . . . You still want to be a teacher one day, right?
You shouldn't stop learning . . . Just come. Maybe you'll like
it . . . or whatever, you don't have to. (*Gesturing to the wounds and
bloody water.*) At least, it will be better than this.

She waits. **Tisana** *says nothing.*

Ruhab   T! –

The call to prayer sounds. **Haleema** *and* **Ruhab** *put on hijabs.*

Haleema (*to* **Ruhab**)   Leave her. I think this stubborn
donkey (*Gesturing to* **Tisana**.) is beginning to enjoy her daily
beatings.

Tisana *opens her mouth but says nothing.*

Haleema (*to* **Tisana**)   Because only *your* God knows why
you won't just say a few words – that you don't have to mean,
go for prayers, like the rest of us and put an end to this all,
before they put a cane in both of our hands – (*Gesturing to herself
and* **Ruhab**.) and make *us* flog you to death! Your face is
ruining my appetite more and more every day.

She exits.

Ruhab *places a hand on* **Tisana**'s *shoulder.* **Tisana** *flinches – it
hurts.*

Ruhab *exits.*

Tisana *stares in the mirror. For a while.*

She looks for something to do. She considers picking bugs out of the garri. It is not her turn, so she doesn't. She picks something up from the floor. She speaks into it like a microphone.

Tisana (*with a finger in her ear, mimicking an American news reporter*) 'Thank you, Phillip. I am all the way in this beautiful, exotic location . . . Here with Mr and Mrs Danja, the parents of the now famous, Tisana. Mr Danja, you must be so proud of your daughter.'

She gets into the role-play. She becomes increasingly excited and carried away by it. She flinches every time she is reminded of the pain she is in. She adopts her father's demeanour.

(*Mimicking her dad.*) 'Mercy, I can't even describe how I feel, proud does not even cut it. When she was returned to us, I thought I could not be happier, but to hear the stories from other girls, to read their letters of thanks, telling how Tisana was brave and stuck to her convictions, how she would pray for them and recite the quotes she had memorised from the Bible. My daughter, the martyr, the *living* martyr.'

She shakes off her dad. She becomes the reporter.

(*Mimicking the reporter.*) 'And Mrs Danja, how do you feel to have her home?'

She stuffs some of the rags in her top. She gives herself large breasts.

(*Mimicking her mum.*) 'She has always been my favourite child. I know a mother shouldn't say such things, but it's true. Ever since she was little, she has always been very obedient . . . very well-behaved. And very beautiful . . . so beautiful. People didn't see how pretty she was before, but since she has been home, everybody now agrees that she is, in fact, the prettiest girl in town . . . maybe even in the country.'

She rips out the stuffing in her top. She sticks a finger in her ear. She listens intently.

(*Mimicking the reporter.*) 'Mrs Danja, I'm getting some news coming in on my ear piece, hold on . . . Yes . . . yes, I can indeed confirm, that the data is in, and Tisana is in fact, *officially*, the prettiest girl on the continent. Congratulations.'

She opens her mouth wide and echoes a whispered 'ahhhh', to imitate the sound of a cheering crowd.

She stuffs rags down the left side of her top. She turns to her right.

(*Mimicking her mum.*) 'Excellent.'

She turns to her left.

(*Mimicking her dad.*) 'Excellent'.

She turns to the front and pulls out the rags.

(*Mimicking the reporter.*) 'Excellent'.

Scene Ten

Interior. **Haleema** *and* **Ruhab** *are occupied with chores.*

Haleema   Ask him.

Ruhab (*irritated*)   No, Haleema.

Haleema   He's not like them, right? He's on our side, right? You said. So ask him.

Ruhab   They'll kill him . . . and then they'll kill us.

Haleema   Not if they don't catch us –

Ruhab   – Haleema, no. Stop. I told you, forget that stupid plan. You will get us all killed. He –

Haleema   – If he is so good, why are you so afraid to ask him? If he really cares about you, surely he'll tell us the patrol rota, surely he will want to help. If he is so nice, why wouldn't he want you to be free, why wouldn't he want you to be safe, to be happy –

Ruhab   – I *am* happy!

I mean . . .

Haleema   It's OK. I know what you mean. It's fine. I won't ask again. Forget it.

Ruhab   You too . . . Forget it, OK? Please Halle. We're OK . . . aren't we? We're together . . . The three of us. As long as we're together . . .

Haleema *forces a smile. She nods at* **Ruhab***, who forces herself to believe* **Haleema***'s smile.*

Ruhab *picks up the mirror. She looks into it. She gets ready. She makes an extra effort to be well-presented. She puts on lip balm.* **Haleema** *watches her.* **Ruhab** *feels* **Haleema** *watching. She is uncomfortable. Guilty, maybe. Embarrassed, maybe.*

Ruhab (*uncomfortable, deflecting*)   That Glory, she's a crook. The things I had to give up, for this . . . And it's almost finished – she never told me that. (*Smiling at her reflection.*) It was worth it, though.

Haleema *watches* **Ruhab***, who tries not to look at her.*

Ruhab   I don't even want to know where she's been hiding it.

She smells the container.

I really don't want to know.

Haleema *watches* **Ruhab***.*

Haleema   Are you staying with him tonight?

Ruhab *looks at* **Haleema***. For a second. She looks away, quickly. She is offended / embarassed.*

Ruhab   Of course not, Halle.

Haleema *watches* **Ruhab***, who tries not to look at her.*

Haleema   You know I don't sleep well . . . So I know when you haven't been here.

Ruhab *slows. She tries not to look at Halle.*

Haleema   You should just be careful . . . You know . . . You know what it's like for the girls that are . . . that they don't think are good – pure.

Ruhab   I should go. I'll see you later.

Scene Eleven

Interior. **Haleema, Tisana** *and* **Ruhab** *sleep.* **Haleema** *gets up slowly. She is careful not to wake the others. She retrieves the thing she was making / sharpening. She continues to make / sharpen it.* **Ruhab** *stirs.* **Haleema** *quickly lies down. She pretends to sleep.*

Ruhab *sits up. She feels nauseous. She wants to be sick. She tries to hold it in. She is going to be sick. The sick rises up into her throat.*

Haleema's *'thing' drops. The sick is in* **Ruhab**'s *mouth. They both freeze.* **Ruhab** *swallows the vomit.* **Haleema** *convincingly pretends to snore.*

Ruhab *holds her tummy gently. She rubs it. She smiles. She kisses her hand. She touches her stomach. She smiles. She lays down. She holds / rubs her stomach.*

They all 'sleep'. For a moment.

Haleema *pops her head up. She looks around. She checks the others are asleep. She hides her 'thing'.*

Scene Twelve

Interior. **Haleema** *is huddled in a corner / by her hiding place. She is doing something. We can't see what.*

Ruhab *and* **Tisana** *enter. They carry a bucket of water each.*

Tisana *is covered with bruises. She looks worse than ever.*

Tisana (*while entering*)   I-C-E-V-E. Receive.

Ruhab   How can I test you when I don't even remember the correct spellings myself?

She notices **Haleema**.

Tisana   Come on, one mo –

Ruhab (*to* **Haleema**)   – What are you doing?

Haleema *hides whatever it is she is doing.*

Haleema   Nothing.

Ruhab   You have been very quiet recently. One might even say, *suspicious.*

Haleema   What are you talking about? You are just bored.

Ruhab   Show me your hands.

Tisana   Ru, leave her.

Ruhab   Go on, show me your hands.

Haleema *raises her hands. She is smug/petulant. Her hands are empty.*

Something falls to the ground. **Ruhab** *dives on to the floor to retrieve it.* **Haleema** *tries to tackle her. They tussle for a moment.*

Tisana   Ru, just leave her alone.

Ruhab (*screaming*)   No! What's she hiding?

Haleema (*grunting*)   Mind your own damn business.

She and **Ruhab** *separate. They pant.* **Ruhab** *has what she was fighting for. It is some sort of shiv.*

Ruhab   What is this?

Haleema   It's mine.

She reaches for the shiv.

Give it to me.

Ruhab *moves the shiv out of* **Haleema***'s reach.*

Ruhab   No. What the hell, Haleema? What are you planning to do with this?

Haleema   What do you think?

Ruhab   Finally cut your toenails, I hope.

Haleema   Give it to me.

Ruhab   No way. You think you'll get far with this?

Haleema   Well, we'll see, won't we?

Ruhab   No! What we'll see is your body on top of the heap of rotting corpses out there, before dawn.

Tisana   Halle, she's right. They –

Haleema   – Shut up, T.

Ruhab   Don't tell her to shut up.

Haleema   You can shut up too.

Ruhab   *You* shut up!

Tisana   Both of you shut up!

They all freeze. For a second. All equally surprised at **Tisana** *(including herself). She cowers slightly.*

(*Taking courage.*) Ruhab, give it back to her.

Ruhab *doesn't move.*

Tisana   Give it to her. You know we cannot stop Haleema from doing what she wants to do. Nobody can. Not since she was a child, and not now. If she says she is going to escape, with that toy, then that is exactly what she will do. And if by some miracle of Christ she makes it, and they don't cut off her hands for raising them with a knife, then excellent. And if they flog us to death, or stick us in a hole shoulder deep, and have the children throw stones at our head, until even our own mothers will be unable to recognise our bodies for burial – because they will assume that we aided her escape, then so be it. If that is the price so that one of us will be free . . . then so be it.

They stand in silence. For a while.

Ruhab   Fuuuuuuck thaaat!

She snaps the shiv and tucks it in her waist band.

I'm dropping it in the well on the way to prayers.

Haleema   Bitch.

Both of you.

Tisana   What did *I* do?

Haleema   That stupid reverse psychology bullshit speech. Do you think I am a fool . . . that that would actually work on me?

Tisana (*quietly*)   I guess we'll never know.

Haleema   What do you want from me?

Ruhab   To not get us all killed.

Tisana   To be patient.

Haleema (*in an outburst*)   There's no time for patience. Any day now they are coming for us. For me, and for you, T. They will ship us away, to different places, or they will strap a bomb to us and send us to –

Tisana   – What? –

Haleema   – A bomb. (*Demonstrating.*) Boom. Boom. Ahh ahh –

Tisana   – I know what a –

Haleema   – Ru told me –

Tisana   – Ru? –

Haleema – Yes, or they will sell us –

Ruhab – No! I'm working something out. You can be safe . . .
T . . . you'll marry 'Tall Arab' –

Haleema – You what?!

Tisana – What?! No . . . (*To herself.*) I can't.

Ruhab He is strong, and he is wise. He is respected. And I
have seen him be kind. It is not a bad choice.

Tisana I can't . . .

Ruhab You will . . . you have to.

Haleema No. She doesn't. You – You're – She's not yours
to give away!

Tisana I just mean . . . maybe I'm . . .

Ruhab (*to* **Haleema**) You're just angry because you're not
in charge any more –

Haleema – I wish, for a second, I didn't have to be in charge
– that you fools could look after yourselves.

Ruhab From where I'm standing, Halle –

Haleema – From where *I'm* standing, Ruhab, you're
married! You are married . . . not pretend like with Moses . . .
married! And she . . . she is losing her mind. And I'm the only
one trying to save us –

Ruhab – No. *I'm* trying to save us. You're going to get us
killed! You don't have the answers any more.

Haleema You think this is the answer? Giving her away to –
letting him – she hasn't even had a period. We're still childr –

Ruhab – It's not like that! . . . Not everything is about . . .
She won't have to . . . It just means we'll be safe. Together.

Haleema For God's sake, Ruhab.

Tisana Maybe I'm too young, and I'm not really –

Ruhab (*to* **Tisana**)   – I've told them that I will get you ready.

Tisana   Ru . . .

Haleema   Who *are* you?

Where has Ruhab gone?

Tisana *steps away. She sits quietly in a corner. She picks at her wounds and scars. She mutters to herself. She shakes her head.* **Ruhab** *and* **Haleema** *forget she is there.*

Ruhab   I'm right here.

Haleema   No . . . This is Ishy's wife . . . not our Ru . . . Actually – maybe . . . Yes . . . actually . . . I guess you got what you've *always* needed – Even here – For some boy to choose you, to tell you that you're the prettiest girl –

Ruhab   – So that's what this is about. It's not my fault that you're ugl –

Haleema   – That's why you stalled my plan, isn't it? So they would marry you off to Ishy and you could ride off into the sunset together with matching Klash-ni-koffs and the blood of infidels dripping from your his-and-her machetes.

Ruhab   You scold T for being beaten and scold me for avoiding it. Don't you dare judge me for surviving. I will do what I have to. This is it. This is our lot.

And he is a good man.

Haleema   Good? He has the words, 'Kill them wherever you find them', carved into his arms. *Carved.*

Ruhab   If we flicked through the Old Testament –

Haleema   – It's not about the scriptures – and what happened to it's 'all the same God' – whatever. It's not about *any* book – *carved. Carved!* With a knife, for goodness sake.

Ruhab   He –

Haleema   – Is a monster too. Maybe he was good before. I'll give you the benefit of the doubt. But they've turned him into a monster, just like they're turning –

Ruhab   – We are here. Do you want me to be like you, fighting in my mind every day, or like T, letting them use my body as a whipping tree?

Haleema   I just want you to stay on *our* side.

Ruhab   There are no sides any more! Get it through your head. They have won, and we are the prize.

Haleema   I am nobody's prize –

Ruhab   – Only because nobody wants you. Your mother didn't, they don't, nobody wants you, and you're taking it out on me!

Haleema   You silly silly little girl. You think Ishy *wants* you? That that man *desires* you? How long has he been here and he is already on what . . . wife number three . . . *four*? He has probably savaged the vaginas of all his other wives to the point of no elasticity, so the monster that he is, just like the dogs back home, has set his eyes on the weakest, smallest, most *broken* bushrat . . .

But you think what you need to . . . To *survive*.

Haleema *and* **Ruhab** *stare at each other.*

Ruhab *pulls out the broken shiv pieces and slams them on the table.*

Ruhab   Take it. Escape. I hope you make it. Or I hope they catch you. I just hope you are gone. Soon. For good.

She exits.

Haleema *exits, in the opposite direction.*

Tisana's *hands are covered in blood. She picks at her wounds and scars. She cries out/shrieks/screams, over and over, in pain and in tears. She looks from one exit to the other. Back and forth.*

Scene Thirteen

Interior. **Tisana** *watches an imaginary TV. She has an imaginary remote in her hand. She laughs hysterically.*

Ruhab *and* **Haleema** *enter from different sides of the stage. They scowl at each other. They look away. They notice* **Tisana**. *They are unsure of what is going on.*

Haleema   T?

Tisana   Stewie is such a funny baby. Do they know he can talk? And how did they let him leave the country, by himself, with a dog?

She laughs hysterically.

(*To* **Haleema** *and* **Ruhab**.) Have you seen this one?

She laughs.

Tisana   Honestly, the funniest thing I have *ever* seen. Oh gosh. Look. Look look look.

She laughs.

That was funny, right? Guys? It was funny. Come on, you must admit.

Ruhab *and* **Haleema** *look at each other.*

Tisana (*almost pleading, through the laughter*)   Guys? It was funny . . . right?

Haleema *sits next to* **Tisana**. **Ruhab** *follows.*

Haleema   You have shit taste in TV. Give me this.

She grabs the imaginary remote. She changes the channel. She grabs **Ruhab**'s *hand. They climb into the imaginary TV.*

They begin performing.

Haleema   'You're not my mum!'

Ruhab   'Yes. I am!'

Haleema *and* **Ruhab** (EastEnders *theme tune*)   Dun. Dun. Dun. Dun. Dun. Du du dun. Na na na na naaaa

Tisana *gasps and claps. She changes the channel.*

Haleema   'Stephanie, will you accept this rose?'

Ruhab (*as a southern belle*)   'Why, I would be absolutely delighted to.'

Tisana *changes the channel.*

Haleema   'And . . . the award for best performance in a hostage or ransom video goes to . . . (*Opening an imaginary envelope.*) Ruhab!'

Ruhab *grabs her chest in shock and delight.*

Tisana *laughs.*

Ruhab   'I would just like to thank the cameraman for getting my best angles, and God, for giving me these blessed angles to begin with.'

Tisana *changes the channel.*

Haleema *and* **Ruhab** *act out a loud, over-the-top and embarrassing sex scene.* **Tisana** *quickly tries to change the channel. It doesn't change.*

Haleema (*to* **Tisana**)   Sorry, batteries are dead.

She returns to the scene. She and **Ruhab** *are laughing at* **Tisana**'s *embarrassment.*

Tisana *gets up to change the TV at the set. She does.* **Ruhab** *pulls her into the TV.*

Ruhab   'Welcome to *Pop Idol*.'

Tisana *sings and dances around. The other girls join in.*

Tisana's *wounds bleed through her shirt.* **Ruhab** *and* **Haleema** *both notice. They look at each other. They turn away from each other. They are still angry. They keep a smile on their faces, for* **Tisana***.*

Scene Fourteen

Interior. **Ruhab** *tends to* **Tisana**'s *wounds.* **Tisana** *sews/cleans garri.* **Ruhab** *pauses. She winces. She holds her stomach. The baby kicks. She hasn't felt it before. She wants to tell her friend. She can't. She doesn't.*

Scene Fifteen

Interior. **Haleema** *and* **Tisana** *sort through garri.*

Tisana   I expected some sort of sound to come out of him. Like maybe it was trapped and . . . and the fire . . . like, when the fire makes the pot hiss and sing, when Mama is cooking.

Bawa, I mean.

Haleema   He was a mute.

Tisana   But still. I thought maybe the sound was trapped.

People weren't good to him. I felt sorry for him.

Haleema   I'm sure he feels sorry for us now. (*Looking up.*) Wherever he is. I wish I was –

Tisana   – Don't say that. God forbid.

Haleema   'God' – 'God' – 'God'.

Maybe He's busy – God . . . I don't know what He's doing,
but maybe there are people suffering more than us, more than
Bawa . . . Who knows what is happening on the other side
of the world, in villages, in cities, in places we don't even
know of . . .

Tisana   Maybe.

She picks bugs out of the garri. She concentrates hard.

You know what, when we go home, I will never eat chicken
again. All the smell of chicken in the air . . . every time I smell
it, I will think of him – think of Bawa.

Haleema   We have to go. Soon.

Tisana   But –

Haleema   – T! Come on. Look around. Girls are disappearing.
Every day the queue to the food is smaller, there are less
people on the girls' side of prayer. Where do you think they
have gone?

Tisana   Maybe . . .

Haleema   Amara said they dragged her little sister from her
arms, while they were sleeping. The middle of the night . . .

Tisana   Let's talk to Ru. We can –

Haleema   – You can't talk to Ru.

She's not one of us any more. We can't trust her.

Tisana   I –

Haleema   – The other day –

Tisana   – They made her –

Haleema – No, T. Well, yes. But. T. She believes it. All of it. She held that whip in her hand. She didn't cry. She didn't close her eyes. She looked at what she was doing and she didn't cry. She didn't throw up. And you know what she's like – what she used to be like. She would have cried. She would have been sick everywhere. She believes it.

Tisana No . . . They made her . . .

Haleema *shakes her head.*

Tisana I can't leave Ru.

Haleema And I can't stay.

Tisana We said –

Haleema – We were children –

Tisana – Together forever, Halle. We said.

Haleema (*quietly*) Please don't make me go without you.

She shakes her head. She is tired. She gives up.

You have to look after yourself now, OK? It's time to grow up. No more pretend play, OK? You have to be here. Your mind has to be here, Tisana.

She goes to a corner. She digs into a gap in the wall, with her fingers.

She returns to **Tisana.**

Haleema Here.

She hands **Tisana** *a shiv.*

Haleema I made you one.

Tisana *doesn't take it.*

Haleema Don't be a pussy.

Tisana Halle.

Haleema   Take it.

She shoves the shiv into **Tisana**'s *hand. It cuts her.*

Tisana   Ow.

Haleema   Good. So you know it's sharp. Now you know what it can do. If you need it. Use it.

You're not safe here, you know. She won't – she *can't* protect you . . .

Tisana *returns to sorting garri.*

Haleema   Ruhab . . . She – If she – Make sure you use that if you have to . . . On *whoever* you have to.

Tisana *looks at* **Haleema**. *For a moment. She is unsure if she understands what she is suggesting.*

Tisana   You're going soon?

Haleema *nods*

Tisana   When?

Haleema   If you're not coming, I can't tell you –

Tisana   – I won't –

Haleema   – I know . . . but you're not a good liar . . . and I don't want you getting hurt because of me . . .

Tisana   Will you go back home?

Haleema   I doubt anyone will be there. One of the new girls told me that she knows our village and there's really nobody left. Those that survived are probably in camps somewhere . . . Who knows where . . . I might try and cross the river . . . I'll find a way . . .

Tisana   Do you think we'll ever see them again? People from home?

Haleema   I doubt it. There are millions of people scattered everywhere. It would be like dropping a bottle of salt on the sand and trying to find every grain.

Tisana *is still. She is sad.* **Haleema** *watches her.*

Haleema   Maybe . . . maybe we'll see them again.

Tisana *brightens.*

Tisana   I think the UN will help. They'll have camps and registers and people from England and France and places like that, that can help us find people. They'll have lists –

Haleema   – T. They . . .

She sees the pleading in **Tisana**'*s face. She changes her mind.*

Haleema   OK. Maybe.

You should come with me.

Tisana   I am not brave, like you. I'm scared . . .

Haleema   Tisana, you are the bravest person I have *ever* known.

She pulls up **Tisana**'*s clothes to reveal her scars.*

Haleema   This. It's not the marks of a coward. You are braver than us all.

Tisana *is uncomfortable. She is embarrassed. She covers up.*

Haleema   Imagine what Aiyi is doing now, or Ladi, or Jumai . . . (*To herself.*) We should have jumped from the trucks when they did.

. . . Maybe the UN has found their families –

Let's –

Tisana   – If Ruhab comes –

Haleema   – No –

Tisana   – I'm not leaving without her –

Haleema   – She won't –

A call for prayer sounds. **Haleema** *puts on her hijab. She goes to leave. She stops.*

Don't say anything to her.

Tisana   But –

Haleema   – Let me think about it first.

She exits.

Scene Sixteen

Interior. **Haleema** *and* **Tisana** *sleep. Noise is heard outside. A flashlight is seen through the cracks.* **Tisana** *wakes. She wakes* **Haleema**.

Tisana (*whispering*)   Halle. Halle.

Haleema *wakes. She sees the light. She covers* **Tisana**'s *mouth.*

Haleema   Shh.

Tisana   Halle. They're going to take –

Haleema   – Shh. It's OK.

The light and the sounds get closer, seem to hover by their door.

Haleema *scrambles for her knife. Quietly she finds it. She searches for* **Tisana**'s *knife. She finds it. She hands it to* **Tisana**. **Tisana** *takes it. They both stand, in a pose, as if ready to attack. They look strong, like warriors, though they tremble and tears stream down* **Tisana**'s *face. They hold one another's hand.*

The noise outside moves on. The lights move. A girl is heard screaming nearby. The screams and the sounds of a truck fade into the distance.

Scene Seventeen

Haleema *and* **Tisana** *nod in and out of/fight against sleep. They are propped up. They hold hands. They cling on to their shivs.*

Scene Eighteen

Interior. **Haleema**, **Tisana** *and* **Ruhab** *sit around the table.* **Tisana** *and* **Haleema** *look tired. There is still tension between* **Haleema** *and* **Ruhab**.

Ruhab   I can't.

Tisana   Why not? She has a plan – a good plan.

Ruhab   My husband will look for me. He won't stop until –

Haleema (*to* **Tisana**)   – See. I told you. Now we can't go. I told you.

Ruhab (*to* **Tisana**)   But, T . . . If you believe in this plan . . . If you think it will work, go . . .

Haleema (*to* **Ruhab**)   So you can tell them –

Ruhab (*to* **Haleema**)   – You think I would do that? To T? To *you*? I'm still me. (*To* **Tisana**.) I still love you – (*To* **Haleema**.) both of you.

Ruhab   We've always been very different people. We've always believed different things about the world. But we've always loved each other. We will always protect each other. Right?

Everything I have done . . . whatever you think of me . . .

She sighs.

I am at peace with it all – the things I have done. That is between me and Allah . . . We're all just trying to live the best way we know how . . . to make the world the best we think it

should be . . . to be pleasing to God . . . We're not perfect –
none of us . . . We're all just trying . . . aren't we? But you have
to know . . . I will *always* protect you. Both of you. Against
whoever and whatever you feel you need protecting from . . .
Against God Himself, if I have to. Always.

Tisana *holds both of their hands.*

Tisana (*to* **Ruhab**)   Please . . . come.

Haleema *reaches out and holds* **Ruhab**'s *hand.*

Haleema (*to* **Ruhab**)   Ru . . . Please . . . Come with us . . .

*They sit in silence. For a moment. Feeling connected. More than they
have felt in a while.*

Ruhab *lets go of their hands.*

Ruhab   I can't –

Haleema   – Yes / –

Tisana   / Ru / –

Ruhab   / – I'm pregnant.

Haleema *and* **Tisana** *look at* **Ruhab**'s *belly. They sit in silence.*

Haleema   You don't have to . . . You know, you don't have
to keep it –

Tisana   – Haleema.

Haleema   What?! I don't have time to debate the details of
my morality and conscience with you. The world we are in
right now does not permit –

Tisana   – No matter what this world looks like, that baby –

Haleema   – That thing inside of her – that thing is not – it's
the devil.

Tisana   / Haleema!

Ruhab   / Halle.

Haleema   It's true. You know that we are our father's
children, before anything else. And its father is the devil. (*To*
Ruhab.) You are carrying the devil.

Ruhab   Stop it. Stop. Stop saying that!

Haleema   I just don't want you to have to go through
something because you think it's *right*. There is no more right
or wrong, it is all just wrong or wrongest.

They say that if you make yourself really hot and put
something sharp inside –

Tisana   – No no no no no please. (*To* **Ruhab**.) Don't listen
to her. Above anything else, it is dangerous.

Ruhab (*to* **Haleema**)   I have no family left . . . nothing to
go back for. (*To* **Tisana**.) You have hope that your family is
alive . . . (*To* **Haleema**.) Your dad was out to town that day,
so maybe he's safe. I watched my house burn to the ground.

Tisana   Maybe they weren't inside.

Ruhab   And maybe they were . . . I just don't have the
energy to make myself believe the impossible, like you do, T.

Tisana   Well, you can still come with us – you *and* the baby –
we'll be together – *we* are your family. We can take a bag of
garri so you won't be hungry.

Haleema   And you can wear my slippers – they're more
comfortable.

Ruhab *looks at* **Haleema** *tenderly.*

Ruhab   And when I start to show? What then? People will
know exactly where the baby has come from. (*Holding her belly.*)
They will reject us both.

Tisana   But if we find your mum –

Ruhab   – It is better to be dead, than to make her ashamed.
If my family is alive, then they have probably mourned me
already. Why make them dig up my grave, only to wish every
day that I was dead. They won't understand . . . They will only
understand their shame . . . Why would I leave here? Here,
where I am my husband's pride, to return to a place where
I will be my father's shame?

I'm sorry . . . but I can't go with you . . . I don't *want* to. I have
a purpose now. I have a family now. I am blessed beyond
measure . . . I lost everything and now I think I might have
everything again. (*Placing a hand on her stomach.*) Alhamdulillah.

But you go. If that's what you want.

She digs a piece of paper out of her underwear. She unfolds it.

Half the men are off training somewhere. We – they . . . *We*
have lost strongholds, and supply routes have been choked so
there is a big push to claim back territory, many chapters are
stretched . . . Sometimes there are fewer patrols when the men
go for supplies . . . This is their rota. (*Pointing to the paper.*)
That's when you should go. If you run west, you won't cross
their path. Don't stop in the next village, they are against the
military, so they pledge us their support. They will betray you.
Do not stop there. I will stay with Ishy, I will tell him to stay
with me because the baby is making me sick. (*Smiling to herself.*)
He will stay. He says I am his queen and my wish is his
command. So when they ask me about you, I can say I don't
know, that I wasn't here. And my husband will swear he was
with me all night.

Tisana *opens her mouth to speak. Nothing comes out.* **Ruhab** *holds
their hands.*

I'll be OK . . . Time I started looking after myself, right Halle?

Ruhab *smiles at* **Haleema**. *Playfully. Halle can't smile back.*

Ruhab   We'll all be OK. Better than OK . . . I'll be a hot mum . . . (*To* **Tisana**.) And you'll teach something boring, at Harvard. (*To* **Haleema**.) And . . . I don't know, you'll be a lesbian or something.

Tisana *laughs.*

Haleema   I'm joking . . . You'll be something great . . . The *greatest* lesbian of all time . . . better than Ellen Degeneres.

Haleema *punches* **Ruhab** *in the arm.*

Ruhab   Ow . . . I'm playing.

You'll be a hero . . . You'll carry on being a hero.

(*Teasing.*) I think my plan might be better than Halle's, T . . . What do you think?

They laugh a little. They squeeze each other's hands.

Scene Nineteen

Interior. **Haleema** *and* **Tisana** *fiddle and fuss. We can't see over what. They are quiet and suspicious.*

Ruhab *enters.*

Tisana   Surprise!

Ruhab *jumps.*

Ruhab   God's sake. Shit . . . I think I pissed a little.

Tisana   Sorry.

Ruhab   No, it's the baby. I'm always peeing myself.

Haleema   Ew!

Tisana (*excited, to* **Ruhab**)   Come and look.

Ruhab *heads over to the girls.*

Ruhab   What is this?

Tisana   Your baby shower! –

Ruhab *is touched.*

Haleema   – It was Tisana's idea.

Tisana (*handing* **Ruhab** *a newspaper wrapped package*)   *She* made this for you.

Ruhab   Halle . . .

Haleema   Just . . .

Haleema *is embarrassed.* **Ruhab** *hugs her tightly.* **Ruhab** *unwraps the parcel. It is a black t shirt. It is tiny.*

Haleema   It's not very festive. It's the only material I –

Ruhab   – Halle. I love it! Black is slimming. And you've seen my husband, this baby will need to be on a diet, like immediately!

Tisana (*to* **Ruhab**)   Look how good her sewing is now.

Ruhab   It's beautiful.

Tisana   OK. My turn. My turn.

She shoves another package into **Ruhab**'s *hands.* **Ruhab** *unwraps.*

Ruhab   Choco Miloooo! My favourite. How did you even get –

Tisana   – Well, Halle hooked it up.

Ruhab   Guys –

I'm going to miss you guys.

Tisana (*placing a hand on* **Ruhab**'s *belly*)   We're going to miss *you* guys.

Haleema   Alright alright, enough of this mushy crap.

She begins singing a song. **Tisana** *and* **Ruhab** *join in. They try to remember the dance they made up to accompany the song. They laugh. They dance. They sing.*

The lights fade. As they do, **Ruhab**'s *moves become laboured. A twinge in her stomach.*

Ruhab (*clutching her stomach*)   Ah!

Haleema *and* **Tisana** *continue to dance and sing.*

Ruhab   Ahh . . .

Haleema *stops.*

Haleema   What? What is it?

Ruhab   I don't know. Ahhhh . . .

Tisana (*quietly*)   Ruhab.

Ruhab   Ahh.

Haleema   Ru. Sit down.

Ruhab   Ahhhhhhh ah ahhhh . . .

She is panting, in pain. She sits. She screams. A red patch spreads across her dress.

No. No. No no no. / Please. Please. Please please please –

Haleema   – T. T, get some water. / Get something.

Tisana *freezes.*

Ruhab   / No no no. Ahhhhhhh ah. Please, Halle. Hall, help me.

Haleema   I'm here, I've got you. You're OK.

Scene Twenty

Interior. **Haleema** *holds* **Ruhab**. *There is a lot of blood. The black T-shirt* **Haleema** *made wraps a small bundle. They stare at it.*

Haleema *looks at* **Tisana** *and* **Ruhab**. *She knows she has to make it better. She can't.*

Tisana   Boy or girl?

They stare at the still bundle.

Ruhab   I . . .

Ruhab *can't get the words out. She shakes her head.*

Haleema   It . . .

Ruhab   I . . .

Tisana   Whatever you want. He or she, can be whoever you want . . . Boy or girl?

Ruhab   Boy. A boy.

Tisana   Good . . . this world is not for girls.

Name?

Ruhab *thinks.*

Ruhab   Moses.

Tisana   Tell us about your son, Moses. What was he like?

Haleema *squeezes* **Ruhab**.

Ruhab   Greedy . . . like his dad . . . My bone structure . . . Mashallah.

She tries to smile.

He was free.

Haleema *quickly wipes a tear.*

Tisana   He is. He is.

Scene Twenty-One

Interior. **Tisana** *and* **Ruhab** *sleep.* **Ruhab** *cries in her sleep.*
Haleema *sits. She is tired. She watches over her friends. She watches the door. She grips her knife tight.*

Scene Twenty-Two

Interior. **Ruhab** *sleeps in* **Haleema***'s lap.* **Haleema** *holds her knife. She sleeps.* **Tisana** *stands. She holds a pose, as if ready to fight. She is tired. She holds her knife. She stares at the door. A light passes. The sound of a truck passes. Movement, noise, shouting is heard. The sounds fade.*

Scene Twenty-Three

Interior. **Tisana** *picks bugs out of the garri.* **Haleema** *tries to plait* **Ruhab***'s hair. She's not very good at it.* **Ruhab** *lies still.*

Scene Twenty-Four

Interior. **Tisana** *does* **Ruhab***'s hair.* **Tisana** *looks tired. She sings.* **Haleema** *picks bugs out of the garri.* **Ruhab** *looks better than before.* **Haleema** *looks even more sleep-deprived.* **Ruhab** *joins in a little with* **Tisana***'s song.*

Tisana (*to* **Ruhab**)   Don't touch it, I'm going to get the mirror.

She looks for the mirror.

Where's the mirror?

She looks under **Haleema**. **Haleema** *doesn't move to assust her.* **Tisana** *finds it. She gives* **Haleema** *a 'thanks for nothing' look.*

She holds the mirror up in front of **Ruhab**.

Tisana   Ta-da.

Ruhab (*with forced enthusiasm, as she checks herself out*)   Tiwa Savage, eat your heart out. Genevieve Nnaji, don't jealous me.

Tisana *hugs* **Ruhab** *tight*.

Scene Twenty-Five

Interior. **Haleema** *prepares their food*.

Tisana   But, what does it *feel* like?

Ruhab   Like the bit of skin that connects your thumb to your pointing finger is being sliced through with a rusty tin lid.

Tisana   No! –

Ruhab   – Yes. And then when I'm on top – I hate being on top – never get on top – start as you mean to go on – sometimes, when I'm on top, I feel like it's going to burst right through my body and come out of my mouth. Like when you scrub too hard and your fingers tear through those plastic gloves for cleaning.

Tisana *gasps*. **Haleema** *laughs*.

Haleema   Wow . . . well at least Ishy and Scarface don't have *that* problem in common. (*Wiggling her baby finger.*) Lucky you.

Ruhab   I am . . . And *not* just because he has a plantain-sized ban –

Tisana   – Ru!

Haleema *and* **Ruhab** *laugh at* **Tisana**.

Ruhab   – but because he thinks I am God's special gift to him. Even after . . .

Tisana   So . . . does it . . . does it feel good at all?

Ruhab   Of course it does. Just not at first. You have to do it loads. Like Aunty Hafsat said . . . (*In Aunty Hafsat's voice.*) 'Practice makes what?'

Tisana *puts her hand up. She pretends to be a student in a classroom.*

Tisana   Ooh, ooh, pick me, miss. I know. I know.

Tisana, **Haleema** *and* **Ruhab** (*in Aunty Hafsat's voice*) 'Practice makes perfection.'

They laugh.

Ruhab (*to* **Haleema**)   You ready?

Haleema   Yeah –

Tisana   – Should we pray? Tonight. Before we go. I mean . . . Pray together?

Haleema   To who?

Tisana   God.

Haleema   Your God? Her God? . . . Womba?

(*To* **Rahab**.) Will you . . .

Ruhab   I'll be OK here. Trust me . . . I thought he treated me like a queen before . . . But *now* – (*Thinking.*) what's better than a queen?

Tisana   Beyoncé?!

Ruhab   Now, he treats me like Beyoncé! . . . When I am better, he says we will try again . . . I'm happy, believe me . . . He is my home.

Now promise me –

Haleema   – I know. We won't stop until –

Ruhab   – Good. The second village.

She retrieves something. It is wrapped up. She hands it to **Haleema**.

Here.

Haleema   What's this?

Ruhab   Open it.

Haleema *unwraps it. It is a knife. A proper one.* **Haleema** *is touched. She shakes off the emotion. She tries to make a joke.*

Haleema   My favourite.

Ruhab   Halle . . . –

Haleema   – I know.

Ruhab   Those shit toy kni –

Haleema   – Thank you.

She places their dinner on the table. They join her.

Ruhab   Our last dinner together –

Haleema   – for now.

Tisana   Maybe one day –

Haleema   – *Definitely* one day . . .

Ruhab   I love you guys.

Haleema   Shut up.

Tisana   She loves us too.

They begin to eat. **Haleema** *stops eating. She folds her hands and bows her head.* **Tisana** *and* **Ruhab** *look at one another. They copy* **Haleema**.

Haleema   Dear God, Allah, Womba, and anyone else that cares. Keep us safe until you bring us back to each other.

Tisana (*smiling*)   Amen.

Ruhab   Amen.

Scene Twenty-Six

Interior. It is pitch black. Lights flash, explosions sound.

Scene Twenty-Seven

Interior. Everything, including the girls, is covered with dirt and dust.

Ruhab *sits with her back to us.* **Tisana** *stands in front of* **Ruhab**. *She does* **Ruhab**'s *hair.* **Haleema** *is sitting at the table. Her head is buried in a book.*

There are buckets of water and a half-bag of garri spilling over. **Tisana** *limps as she moves about.*

She laughs.

Tisana (*to* **Ruhab**)   Don't touch it, I'm going to get the mirror.

Limping, she looks for the mirror. She can't find it.

Where's the mirror? Who had it last? Urrr. (*To* **Ruhab**.) Don't move. I'll find it.

She looks around **Haleema**.

Tisana (*quietly*)   Sorry, don't mind me.

She feels under and around **Haleema**.

Tisana   A-ha.

She pulls hard. She retrieves the mirror. She gives **Haleema** *a 'thanks for nothing' look.*

She holds the mirror up in front of **Ruhab**.

Tisana   Ta-da. Look.

She places the mirror in **Ruhab**'s *hand.*

On the table are three bowls. Two of them are piled high. They overflow with garri. The third bowl is empty.

Tisana *serves the same amount of garri into all three bowls.*

Tisana   Dinner, guys.

She shifts **Haleema**, *and takes the book from her. She sits her upright, behind her overflowing bowl.* **Haleema**'s *body falls hard off the chair. It falls to the floor, with a thud.*

Haleema *is dead.*

Tisana   Uh-oh. Be careful.

She lifts **Haleema** *up.* **Haleema** *is heavy.* **Tisana** *struggles. She pops* **Haleema** *back on her chair. She goes to* **Ruhab**.

Tisana   Come on, Miss World, enough looking at yourself. You look beautiful.

She drags **Ruhab**'s *body to the table. She is stiff. She is heavy.*

Ruhab *is dead.*

Tisana *sits* **Ruhab** *upright, behind her overflowing bowl of garri.*

She sits behind her own bowl of garri.

Tisana   Yum. Yum. Yum. Beans, yam and palm oil, my favourite. *Bon-appétit.*

Curtain.

Bloomsbury Methuen Drama Modern Plays
include work by

Bola Agbaje
Edward Albee
Davey Anderson
Jean Anouilh
John Arden
Peter Barnes
Sebastian Barry
Alistair Beaton
Brendan Behan
Edward Bond
William Boyd
Bertolt Brecht
Howard Brenton
Amelia Bullmore
Anthony Burgess
Leo Butler
Jim Cartwright
Lolita Chakrabarti
Caryl Churchill
Lucinda Coxon
Curious Directive
Nick Darke
Shelagh Delaney
Ishy Din
Claire Dowie
David Edgar
David Eldridge
Dario Fo
Michael Frayn
John Godber
Paul Godfrey
James Graham
David Greig
John Guare
Mark Haddon
Peter Handke
David Harrower
Jonathan Harvey
Iain Heggie

Robert Holman
Caroline Horton
Terry Johnson
Sarah Kane
Barrie Keeffe
Doug Lucie
Anders Lustgarten
David Mamet
Patrick Marber
Martin McDonagh
Arthur Miller
D. C. Moore
Tom Murphy
Phyllis Nagy
Anthony Neilson
Peter Nichols
Joe Orton
Joe Penhall
Luigi Pirandello
Stephen Poliakoff
Lucy Prebble
Peter Quilter
Mark Ravenhill
Philip Ridley
Willy Russell
Jean-Paul Sartre
Sam Shepard
Martin Sherman
Wole Soyinka
Simon Stephens
Peter Straughan
Kate Tempest
Theatre Workshop
Judy Upton
Timberlake Wertenbaker
Roy Williams
Snoo Wilson
Frances Ya-Chu Cowhig
Benjamin Zephaniah

Bloomsbury Methuen Drama Contemporary Dramatists

include

John Arden (two volumes)
Arden & D'Arcy
Peter Barnes (three volumes)
Sebastian Barry
Mike Bartlett
Dermot Bolger
Edward Bond (eight volumes)
Howard Brenton (two volumes)
Leo Butler
Richard Cameron
Jim Cartwright
Caryl Churchill (two volumes)
Complicite
Sarah Daniels (two volumes)
Nick Darke
David Edgar (three volumes)
David Eldridge (two volumes)
Ben Elton
Per Olov Enquist
Dario Fo (two volumes)
Michael Frayn (four volumes)
John Godber (four volumes)
Paul Godfrey
James Graham
David Greig
John Guare
Lee Hall (two volumes)
Katori Hall
Peter Handke
Jonathan Harvey (two volumes)
Iain Heggie
Israel Horovitz
Declan Hughes
Terry Johnson (three volumes)
Sarah Kane
Barrie Keeffe
Bernard-Marie Koltès (two volumes)
Franz Xaver Kroetz
Kwame Kwei-Armah
David Lan
Bryony Lavery
Deborah Levy
Doug Lucie

David Mamet (four volumes)
Patrick Marber
Martin McDonagh
Duncan McLean
David Mercer (two volumes)
Anthony Minghella (two volumes)
Tom Murphy (six volumes)
Phyllis Nagy
Anthony Neilson (two volumes)
Peter Nichol (two volumes)
Philip Osment
Gary Owen
Louise Page
Stewart Parker (two volumes)
Joe Penhall (two volumes)
Stephen Poliakoff (three volumes)
David Rabe (two volumes)
Mark Ravenhill (three volumes)
Christina Reid
Philip Ridley (two volumes)
Willy Russell
Eric-Emmanuel Schmitt
Ntozake Shange
Sam Shepard (two volumes)
Martin Sherman (two volumes)
Christopher Shinn
Joshua Sobel
Wole Soyinka (two volumes)
Simon Stephens (three volumes)
Shelagh Stephenson
David Storey (three volumes)
C. P. Taylor
Sue Townsend
Judy Upton
Michel Vinaver (two volumes)
Arnold Wesker (two volumes)
Peter Whelan
Michael Wilcox
Roy Williams (four volumes)
David Williamson
Snoo Wilson (two volumes)
David Wood (two volumes)
Victoria Wood

For a complete listing of Bloomsbury
Methuen Drama titles, visit:
www.bloomsbury.com/drama

Follow us on Twitter and keep up to date
with our news and publications
@MethuenDrama

CPSIA information can be obtained
at www.ICGtesting.com
Printed in the USA
LVHW050001271120
672783LV00012B/254